The Season Starts When?

Cycling Cartoons by O'GRADY

PATRICK O'GRADY

VELOPRESS • BOULDER, COLORADO

For my parents, who left me alone so I could draw, and for Shannon, who didn't.

The Season Starts When?

International Standard Book Number: 1-884737-66-8

Library of Congress Cataloging-in-Publication Data

O'Grady, Patrick, 1954-
The Season Starts When? : a cartoon collection / by O'Grady.
p. cm.
ISBN 1-884737-66-8 (pbk.)
1. Cycling Comic books, strips, etc. I. Title.
PN6727.048S43 1999
741.5'973--dc21 99-31073
CIP

Printed in the USA

Distributed in the United States and Canada by Publishers Group West.

VeloPress
1830 North 55th Street
Boulder, Colorado 80301-2700 USA
303/440-0601; fax 303/444-6788; e-mail velopress@7dogs.com

To purchase additional copies of this book or other VeloPress books, call 800/234-8356 or visit us on the Web at www.velogear.com.

Contents

Dog Breath

VELONEWS
FAT GUYS RULE
IF YOU CAN'T DRAW SOMETHING NASTY ABOUT SOMEONE, TRY, TRY AGAIN
MAD DOG
MEDIA

Curious people always ask cartoonists, "Where do you get your ideas?" When they're not asking, "I suppose you think that crap's funny?" I don't know how my colleagues cerebrate, but my ideas generally arrive shortly after I sacrifice a recreational rider to Satan.

It does thin the herd, what with *VeloNews* up to 20 issues a year and *Bicycle Retailer & Industry News* right on its wheel at 18. And you wondered why USA Cycling's membership numbers keep shrinking.

It's a weird way to earn a living, for sure. I've tried lots of others—janitor, editor, panhandler, reporter—but it's hard to beat scrawling nasty little pictures about people who can't get their hands on you *right now*, while they're still really fried about being depicted as a fat, balding roadie with a pork-rinds sponsor. Or as a mohawked, Band-Aided bicycle mechanic with the I.Q. of a crank bolt. It's kind of like pissing off a bridge after drinking a case of Spare Tire Ale. It's a hard rain's gonna fall, just like Bobby D. promised, and not everyone has an umbrella handy.

It's better to be pissed off than pissed on. And that's why those of us who can draw cartoons. We're pissed off *all the time*, mainly because we're ugly, unskilled and friendless, and we just want to share our feelings with those of you who have lives.

I've been sharing my feelings with an outraged public since my early teens, when I started cartooning for my high school newspaper in Colorado Springs, Colorado. In the three decades since, I've imposed my skewed world view on readers from Vermont to Oregon, as a reporter, editor, columnist and cartoonist for a seemingly endless parade of daily newspapers that finally limped to a halt in 1991, in Santa Fe, New Mexico, when I abandoned the security of a feature editor's salary for the snickering poverty of free-lance journalism in south-central Colorado.

I blame it all on the unholy trinity of John Wilcockson, Felix Magowan and David Walls, who in 1989 declined to hire me as managing editor of *VeloNews*, but suggested that I scratch out a 'toon now and then. That personnel decision worked out nicely for both parties. Inside Communications didn't get driven into bankruptcy by what certainly would have been my bungling of a job that Tim Johnson, now online director of VeloNews Interactive, handled with panache and patience (although I have sent a few advertisers and subscribers shrieking off into the void). And I got to live 90 miles away from the triumvirate referred to fondly by longtime Inside Communications

My very first cycling cartoon, drawn in 1982 when I was a full-time copy editor and part-time cartoonist for the *Corvallis* (Oregon) *Gazette-Times*. I spent a lot of time strolling the Marys and Willamette river trails in various states of consciousness, and considered the omnipresent speeding cyclists to be a pain in the butt. Seventeen years later, I consider pedestrians little more than barely mobile pylons on the slalom course of life. How times do change.

WOW, ARTOO! IT'S DARTH VADER! LET'S GET HIM!
O'GRADY/82 THE GAZETTE-TIMES

employees as "@#?%&!!!," especially on payday.

Thanks, too, to former Sangre de Cristo Cycling Club teammate Mark Sani, who asked me on the Plaza in Santa Fe back in 1991 if I'd be interested in doing a cartoon strip and column for a bicycle-industry magazine he and Bill Tanler were contemplating. I thought he was insane, and so did everybody else, particularly the wizards at all the other trade rags that have done half-gainers into the toilet since *Bicycle Retailer & Industry News* arrived on the trade-mag scene. Bill has since passed on to the Big Office in the Sky, and Marc is trying his hand at consumer journalism with *Bike* and *Powder*, but *Bicycle Retailer* keeps rolling right along.

A tip of the Mad Dog cycling cap as well to *VeloNews*'s technical editor, Charles Pelkey, a keen forward observer whose finely twisted mind has identified a number of legitimate targets for my otherwise indiscriminate fire, which has caused more than its share of collateral damage among editors, readers and advertisers.

And finally, thanks to you for indulging me all these years. *VeloNews*'s Old Guy Who Gets Fat in Winter and *Bicycle Retailer*'s Mud Stud have a few friends holding back that soggy lynch mob under the bridge, and for that I am eternally grateful. Because if it weren't for you, I'd have to get a job.

O'GRADY

Patrick O'Grady
Mad Dog Media Communications Empire
Westcliffe, Colorado
March 1999

ESCAPE
FROM
BEYOND
THE VALLEY
OF THE
PLANET OF THE
FATGUYS!
ONE FOR THE ROAD?
WE'RE CLOSED.
NIGHTCAP?
BEAT IT!
OK, I GET IT... DON'T HAVE TO TELL ME TWICE. I'LL TAKE IT "TO GO."
SAY, AREN'T YOU SUPPOSED TO BE ESCAPING TO SOMEWHERE?
BAR
OLD GUYS WHO GET FAT IN WINT
RACING
SPARE TIRE ALE

WHO IS THE MIGHTY FAT GUY, AND WHERE DID HE COME FROM?
... OUR STORY BEGINS A LONG TIME AGO, IN A GALAXY FAR, FAR... NO, WAIT A MINUTE, THAT'S THE SKINNY KID WITH THE HEAVY-DUTY FLASHLIGHT.
THIS PARTICULAR STORY BEGINS NOT TOO LONG AGO, ON AN ODDLY SHAPED PLANET JUST AROUND THE CORNER...
EAT
MUNCH
CHOMP
GUZZLE
GOBBLE
CHEW
QUAFF
URP
POOT
SCOFF
CHUG
GORGE
BELCH
SWILL

ON THE PLANET WYDELÖDE, EVERYONE'S A TRIFLE STOUT 'CAUSE GRAVITY IS SUCH A BITCH...

GRAVITY'S EXTRA STRONG TODAY, HUH? MORE CHIPS?

TELL ME ABOUT IT... MY 'RHOIDS ARE KILLIN' ME. MORE BEER?

... AND THE STOUTEST OF THEM ALL IS JAR-ALE, WYDELÖDE'S NO. 1 BREWMASTER AND THUS ITS SUPREME LEADER.

ALE TO THE CHIEF!

ACTUALLY, I'D PREFER PORTER.

JAR-ALE AND HIS WIFE, LARDA, HAD A YOUNG SON, KAL-XL, WHO SEEMED SURE TO FOLLOW IN HIS OLD MAN'S FOOTSTEPS (WHICH, GIVEN HIS SIZE, DIDN'T DEMAND MUCH IN THE WAY OF TRACKING).
CHOMP MUNCH CHEW
RIDE TO EAT, EAT TO RIDE.
PIZZA
HONEY? YOU SEEN THE SANDWICH AND BEER I SET OUT FOR LUNCH?
OH, RIGHT, I'M GONNA EAT YOUR SANDWICH WHEN THERE'S A BUNCHA LEFTOVER PIZZA IN...
KAL-XL!
BUT THEN, ONE DAY, JAR-ALE MADE A WEIGHTY PRONOUNCEMENT:
HI, HONEY, I'M HOME. OH, BY THE WAY, OUR PLANET IS DOOMED.
OH, SWELL ... AND ME WITH A CAKE IN THE OVEN.
WE NO LONGER NEED CAKE ... FOR WE SHALL SOON RECEIVE OUR JUST DESSERTS!
WITH THE TYPICAL WYDELÖDIAN NOW WEIGHING MORE THAN TWO OF OUR MOONS, OUR PLANET HAS BEGUN TO COLLAPSE UNDER US... BEFORE LONG, OUR LOVELY DONUT-SHAPED WORLD WILL SHRINK TO THE SIZE OF A DONUT HOLE, WITH CHOCOLATE FROSTING AND MAYBE SOME SPRINKLES AND... (SLURP)... BUT I DIGRESS.
I BUST MY BUTT ON THIS CAKE AND HE'S TALKIN' DONUT HOLES.
LARGE CHARGE. LET'S EAT.

IN SHORT, THERE SOON WILL BE NOTHING TO EAT BUT THE PLANET ITSELF, AND THESE PORKERS WILL GO THROUGH THAT LIKE JUNIOR THERE GOES THROUGH A BUSHEL OF BURRITOS. HELL, I MAY EAT IT MYSELF.
BURRITOS?
UH, YEAH, RIGHT, GOTCHA. SO WHAT'S THE MENU... ER, THE PLAN?

WELL, WE ONLY HAVE THE ONE SPACESHIP LEFT SINCE WE SCRAPPED THE FLEET... CAN'T MAKE BEER CANS AND TV DINNER TRAYS WITHOUT METAL...
I SAY WE USE IT TO SEND KAL-XL TO EARTH... LOTS OF OUR KIND OF FOLKS THERE, IF THEIR "WAL-MARTS" ARE ANY INDICATION.
VISIT
EARTH
FINE
DINING
MILKY WAY
AAA

AND SO, YOUNG KAL-XL BEGINS HIS LONG JOURNEY...
MOMMMM! DAAAD!
HEY, WHAT CAN I SAY? YOU SHOULDA GONE BEFORE YOU LEFT.
KEEP AN EYE OUT FOR STRANGERS WITH CANDY ... YOU'RE GONNA GET HUNGRY...
FWOOM!

THEN, AS JAR-ALE AND LARDA WATCH THEIR ONLY SON ROCKET OUT OF SIGHT...
DO YOU HEAR THAT RUMBLING?
HUH? OH, THAT'S MY STOMACH. WHAT'S FOR DINNER?
RUMBLE

YOUR STOMACH? DINNER? SAYYY... JUST HOW MUCH OF THAT DOOMSDAY STORY OF YOURS WAS HOOEY?
ALL OF IT...
... HEY, THE KID WAS EATING US OUT OF HOUSE AND HOME! I'LL GET YOU A DOG OR SOMETHING. HERE, HAVE A BEER.

WHATEVER: THE YOUNG FAT GUY WAS EN ROUTE TO EARTH. NAVY-SURPLUS SPACECRAFT BEING WHAT THEY ARE, HOWEVER, THE TRIP TOOK THE BETTER PART OF QUITE SOME TIME.
JEEZ, WHO EVER HEARD OF A PLASMA DRIVE WITH A CARBURETOR?
ANY FOOD ON THIS BARGE? LOOKS LIKE SLIM PICKIN'S: LITE BEER, NACHO CHIPS AND BEAN DIP. I HATE FLYING COACH.
LESSEE IF WE CAN PULL IN A LITTLE EARTH TV... HMMM, WHAT'S THIS? TOUR DE FRANCE?

BY THE TIME KAL-XL MADE IT TO EARTH, HE WAS PUSHING 40 IN BOTH YEARS AND WAIST SIZE. PLUS, THE DECADES OF SOLITUDE, THE RAVAGES OF PUBERTY AND WAY TOO MUCH TV HAD FORCED HIM TO DEVISE A SET OF CORRECTIVE LENSES FROM THE BOTTOMS OF TWO BEER BOTTLES.
DON'T BE LOOKIN' FOR NO X-RAY VISION HERE, DUDE...
I NEARLY MISSED THE PLANET... I WAS WATCHING THAT LAST TIME TRIAL IN THE '89 TOUR.
WELCOME TO ROSWELL

HE SOUGHT EMPLOYMENT, BUT AS AN ILLEGAL ALIEN, HE WAS ELIGIBLE ONLY FOR THE MOST MENIAL OF POSITIONS.
AS IT HAPPENS, WE NEED FREE-LANCE JOURNALISTS FOR OUR CYCLING MAG...
...I'M JUST ABOUT OUT OF BEAN DIP!
SAY NO MORE. I'M YOUR MAN WHEN'S LUNCH?

HE EVEN TOOK UP RACING, REASONING THAT HIS MASSIVE WYDELÖDIAN LEGS AND YEARS OF WATCHING THE SPORT ON TV WOULD MAKE HIM A STAR.
BUT THESE EARTH PEOPLE ARE A TRICKY BUNCH.
VELONEWS
FAT CITY!
OLD GUY WINS TOUR!
OLD GUYS WHO GET FAT
SPARE TIRE
SOMEBODY TELL THE SPACE CADET THAT HIS CATEGORY STARTED 10 MINUTES AGO.
FINIS
©O'GRADY 99 MAD DOG MEDIA

More Fat Guys

Deep Fat

It's appropriate that the first cartoon I drew for VeloNews, way back in March 1989, featured the Old Guy Who Gets Fat in Winter Racing Team, a portly sort of a one-man band who always seems to be playing off key. I've long been a big fan of editorial cartoonist Pat Oliphant, who uses his penguinesque alter ego, Puck, as the second half of his one-two editorial punch. Puck is Oliphant; the Old Guy is me.

The Old Guy also serves as a sort of Everyman, wounded seasonally by the slings and arrows of our outrageous sport. Though not every man is amused at the notion of looking like the Old Guy, who has — like his creator —

THE SEASON STARTS WHEN?
OLD GUYS WHO GET FAT IN WINTER RACING TEAM
ALE
O'GRADY '89

gotten gnarlier-looking every year since his birth. I mean, just look at him over there, a mere 10 years later; still spending more time in the chow line than at the start line.

I think of the Old Guy as a sort of Dorian Gray's mirror for myself, and maybe that's why he keeps ballooning up like a shaven-legged Marlon Brando on wheels. Because inside every lithe hill climber is a Guinness-swilling, pork-rind-munching, video-addicted couch spud with a butt so big it needs its own ZIP code.

Trust me. I took up cycling to lose weight after a friend told me I had more chins than the Hong Kong phone book. That well-intentioned insult proved so motivating that in 1993, when I founded a cycling club in Colorado Springs, Colorado, I called it the Old Guys Who Get Fat in Winter Racing Team.

That team, like so many others, has faded off the back and into obscurity. But the Old Guy remains, hungry for more.

More of what? Beer, hoagies, chips...and cycling, of course.

©O'GRADY'89
VELONEWS
WHATRE YOU DOING? THE RACE IS ABOUT READY TO START!
I KNOW. SO SHUDDUP AND SIT DOWN OR YOU'LL MISS IT. GET ME A BEER FIRST.
HI AND WELCOME TO THE TOUR DE FRANCE... I'M JOE GARAGIOLA
OLD GUYS WHO GET FAT IN WINTER RACING TEAM
CHIPOS
TV GUIDE
CYCLING
Patrick O'Grady cartoon

8-4-89 Some things are more important than racing. Like watching other people race. You can drink beer then.

YYAAAARRGH!
HONEY... NOW THAT RACING SEASON'S OVER, I'VE ENROLLED YOU IN A DANCE AEROBICS COURSE. YOU CAN HAVE A STALK OF CELERY FOR LUNCH. LOVE, YOUR WIFE
OLD GUYS WHO GET FAT IN WINTER (BUT LOOK GREAT NOW) RACING TEAM
©O'GRADY '90 VELONEWS
Patrick O'Grady cartoon

9-24-90 One of the few times the Fat Guy wasn't.

THE OFF-SEASON ADVENTURES OF MASTER RACER
BY O'GRADY ©'89 VELONEWS
GOTTA GO TRAIN FOR AN HOUR OR SO, CHIEF.
IN THIS WEATHER? THAT'S WHAT I CALL DEDICATION!
DEDICATION? NAW... IT'S EASY!
YOU JUST HAVE TO DRESS PROPERLY...
OLD GUYS WHO GET FAT IN WINTER RACING TEAM
CLIP CLOP CLIP CLOP
... WARM UP THOROUGHLY...
NNGH
LEAP
CAVORT
TEETER
TOTTER
... AND GET YOUR HEART RATE UP!
OBOY! A FOLDOUT! SLOBBER DROOL
THUMPA THUMPA
VELO FELLOW
THIS ISSUE: BIKES YOU CAN'T AFFORD
Patrick O'Grady cartoon

12-17-90 Think of it as visualization.

AWESOME HOCKEY STOP, DUDE! SKATING LONG?
OH. SHUT UP AND CALL ME A CAB ... AND A NEUROSURGEON...
OLD GUYS WHO GET FAT IN WINTER
GLIDE...
O'GRADY '91 VELONEWS

1-21-91 This must be a long-forgotten teammate. I never looked that good. I skate as well as he does, though.

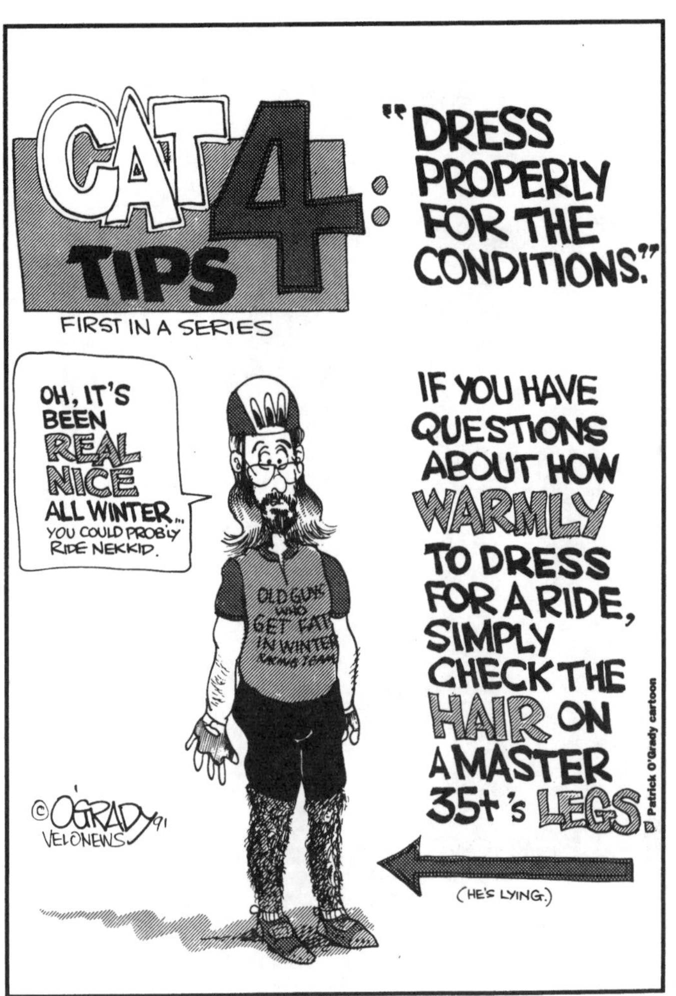

CAT 4 TIPS: "DRESS PROPERLY FOR THE CONDITIONS."
FIRST IN A SERIES
OH, IT'S BEEN REAL NICE ALL WINTER... YOU COULD PROB'LY RIDE NEKKID.
OLD GUYS WHO GET FAT IN WINTER
IF YOU HAVE QUESTIONS ABOUT HOW WARMLY TO DRESS FOR A RIDE, SIMPLY CHECK THE HAIR ON A MASTER 35+'s LEGS.
(HE'S LYING.)
© O'GRADY '91 VELONEWS
© Patrick O'Grady cartoon

3-25-91 Now that's more like it. Like me. Whatever.

MEANWHILE, AT THE MASTERS RACE...
SO YA SET TO RACE, BUDDY?
OH, FOR SURE... I GOT NEW EVERYTHING! NEW SHIFTING SETUP, NEW TITANIUM SADDLE AND FRAME, NEW AERO SKINSUIT, NEW 6oz. HELMET, NEW, NEW, NEW, NEW, NEW YAP YAP YAP YAP YAP YAP YAP BRAG BOAST DECLAIM RAVE...
WHO GET FAT
DEEP POCKETS
... AND AFTERWARD.
SO WHAT HAPPENED?
OLD LEGS... GASP
OLD LUNGS... WHEEZE
SAME OLD STORY... HACK
WEAVE
WOBBLE
©O'GRADY '92 VELONEWS
Patrick O'Grady cartoon

4-20-92 You can't buy love, either.

©O'GRADY '93 VELONEWS
IT'S TRUE (GASP)... PUSHING A FIXED GEAR (WHEEZE) IS GOOD TRAINING! (GROAN)
FASTER... I HAVE A MASSAGE APPOINTMENT.
OLD GUYS WHO GET FAT IN WINTER RACING TEAM
FAT CITY VELO
Patrick O'Grady cartoon

2-8-93 However, you can rent friends with the right amount of beer.

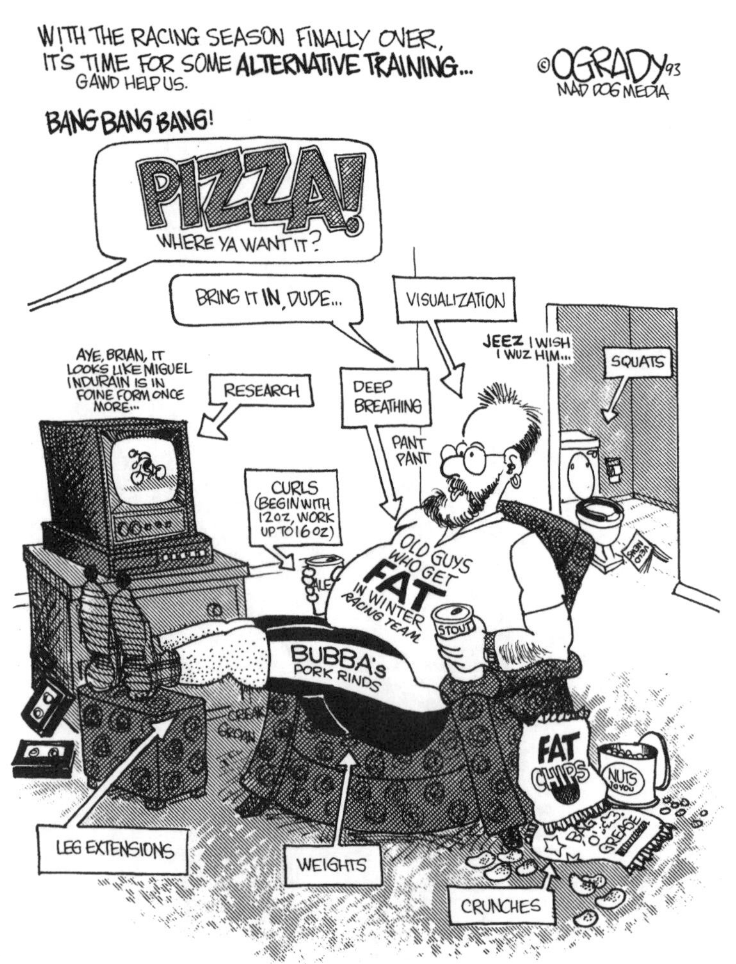
WITH THE RACING SEASON FINALLY OVER, IT'S TIME FOR SOME ALTERNATIVE TRAINING...
GAWD HELP US.
©O'GRADY93 MAD DOG MEDIA
BANG BANG BANG!
PIZZA! WHERE YA WANT IT?
BRING IT IN, DUDE...
VISUALIZATION
JEEZ I WISH I WUZ HIM...
SQUATS
AYE, BRIAN, IT LOOKS LIKE MIGUEL INDURAIN IS IN FOINE FORM ONCE MORE...
RESEARCH
DEEP BREATHING
PANT PANT
CURLS (BEGIN WITH 12 OZ, WORK UP TO 16 OZ)
OLD GUYS WHO GET FAT IN WINTER RACING TEAM
STOUT
BUBBA's PORK RINDS
CREAK GROAN
FAT CHIPS
NUTS
LEG EXTENSIONS
WEIGHTS
CRUNCHES

11-8-93 The original hangs on my office wall. It's disturbingly like a mirror.

BBBRRRRRRRIIIINNNNNGGGG!!! WAKE UP, BUFFALO BUTT! IT'S JANUARY AND TIME TO GET BACK ON THE BIKE!!!
YAAAAAHHHHH!
MY LEG RAZOR!
TILT
WHERE'S MY @#!!! LEG RAZOR?
PIZZA PIT
OLD GUYS WHO GET FAT IN WINTER
TACO HELL
BIKE PORN
EXPENSIVE STOUT
Chips
TV GUIDE TO CYCLING
©O'GRADY94 MAD DOG MEDIA

1-17-94 The seasonal equivalent of "the morning after."

©O'GRADY '94
MAD DOG MEDIA
I HAVE HERE, FROM THE HOME OFFICE IN SIOUX CITY, IOWA, TONIGHT'S TOP 10 LIST ... TOP 10 REASONS WHY GREG LEMOND DOESN'T WIN RACES ANY MORE!
#10-THINKS "FINISH LINE" IS A PRODUCT SPONSORING ANOTHER RIDER AND REFUSES TO CROSS IT...
#9- GETS CLARK-KENT TO BUILD BIKES, BUT NEEDS SUPERMAN...
#8- CAN'T GET THOSE PUDGY ARMS UP IN THE AIR...
#7- KEEPS LOOKING OVER HIS SHOULDER FOR LAURENT FIGNON...
#6- STILL WAITING FOR MIGUEL INDURAIN TO TAKE A PULL...
#5- SPRAINED SHIFTING HAND SIGNING AUTOGRAPHS...
#4- SPRAINED BRAIN ANSWERING STUPID QUESTIONS FROM MAINSTREAM MEDIA...
#3- LOST BET WITH LANCE ARMSTRONG AND MUST CARRY CASE OF SHINER BOCK ON ALL MOUNTAIN STAGES...
#2- HAS BEEN KIDNAPPED AND REPLACED BY LOOK-ALIKE CAT. 5 FROM NEBRASKA...
AND THE #1 REASON... THOSE DARN CARTOONS!
YO, GREG... YEAH, IT'S ME. STILL GOT THAT SPOT OPEN ON THE TEAM... UH HUH... WELL, MAYBE NEXT YEAR, OK? RIGHT...
OLD GUYS WHO GET FAT IN WINTER RACING TEAM
NASTY LEMOND 'TOONS VOL. 66
FAT BURGER

5-30-94 When you watch too much David Letterman, you get fat and develop a thing for top-10 lists.

©O'GRADY '94
MAD DOG MEDIA
ITALIAN CYCLING GREAT GIANNI BUGNO WILL HEAD A TEAM SPONSORED BY MAXWELL HOUSE WHEN HIS SUSPENSION ENDS...
IN RELATED NEWS, THE PIRAHNA HAS BEEN DECLARED AN ENDANGERED SPECIES AS MOUNTAIN BIKERS RAVAGE PET SHOPS FOLLOWING MISSY GIOVE'S VICTORY IN VAIL...
AMAZING WHAT SOME PEOPLE WILL DO TO WIN... HFFFFF...
I'M NOT DEAD YET...
OLD GUYS WHO GET FAT IN WINTER RACING TEAM
GUIDO'S YELLOW LINE APPEALS
BIG MIG™ INHALER

10-3-94 Spends a lot of time in that chair, staring at the TV, huh? Oh, well, at least he's not on dope.

MEANWHILE, NOT TOO FAR DOWN THE ROAD (AS IT WERE)...
AMERICA'S LAST LIVING ROAD RACER, 107-YEAR-OLD KENT BOSTICK, WON THE 2061 U.S. NATIONAL ROAD CYCLING CHAMPIONSHIPS TODAY... HE CLAIMED HIS 40TH STRAIGHT TITLE DESPITE HAVING TO PROMOTE, CONDUCT AND OFFICIATE THE EVENT, HELD ON A WIND TRAINER... LUCKY FOR THE OL' BOY, HE WAS THE ONLY COMPETITOR.
WELL, ISN'T THAT SOMETHING, BOB ... MEANWHILE, IN WASHINGTON, PRESIDENT FURTADO THREW OUT THE FIRST POWERBAR AS THE TOUR OF AMERICA MOUNTAIN-BIKE RACE GOT UNDER WAY...
JUST WAIT 'TIL I REMEMBER WHERE I LEFT MY LICENSE...
...AND MY TEETH...
IT'S COMEBACK TIME!
DEPENDS
BELTONE
ensure
REALLY OLD GUYS WHO USED TO GET FAT IN WINTER BUT DON'T ANY MORE 'CAUSE THE FOOD SUCKS IN THIS LOUSY @#!!!*?! NURSING HOME OUR KIDS (THE BUMS) PUT US IN RACING TEAM
TOOT
©O'GRADY '95 MAD DOG MEDIA

3-13-95 Despite its uplifting message regarding the empowerment of senior citizens, this cartoon obviously is wildly inaccurate in its portrayal of cycling's future. Kent Bostick will not be the only entrant in the 2061 road championships. Ned Overend should be tired of winning off-road triathlons by then....

OFF-SEASON...
GRUNT...
PING
OLD GUYS WHO GET FAT IN WINTER
TWANG
CREAK
SNAP
PRE-SEASON...
WHIRRRRRR
GASSP! WHEEEZE! HORRFF!
OLD GUYS WHO GET FAT ETC.
AND IN-SEASON.
YAY
HURRAH
CHEER
HUZZAH
APPLAUSE
OLD GUYS AND SO ON
HEY, FAT BOY! ISN'T THAT YOUR CATEGORY THAT JUST STARTED?
HUH?
OLD GUYS WHO GET FAT
© O'GRADY '95 MAD DOG MEDIA

5-8-95 A rich fantasy life often leaves you poorer in other respects, usually while people are watching.

HERE IT IS, TIME FOR REDLANDS & CACTUS CUP AND ONCE AGAIN YOU FIND YOURSELF SIMULTANEOUSLY NOWHERE... AND EVERYWHERE.
HEY! I CAN'T FIND MY BIKE!
URP
UH... YOU APPEAR TO BE SITTING ON IT, DUDE.
SHALL I CALL THE PROCTOLOGIST ... AGAIN?
CRREEAAK
THUNDER MUG ALE
WIDE LOAD diner
OLD GUYS WHO GET FAT IN WINTER racing team
triple dip icecream
©O'GRADY '96
MAD DOG MEDIA

4-1-96 April Fool. He's not really sitting on the bike. He's absorbing it.

WELCOME BACK TO OUR COVERAGE OF OLYMPIC CYCLING, BROUGHT TO YOU BY SOMINEX...
Z
© O'GRADY 96 MAD DOG MEDIA
OLD GUYS WHO GET FAT IN WINTER
PORK RINDS

8-5-96 The trouble with cycling on TV is it's cycling on TV.

9-9-96 This was a bit premature, since Ned is still breaking young guys' legs. Still, I'll hoist a mug to him anytime.

BEFORE
"LYCRA POWER"...
URP
OLD GUYS WHO GET FAT IN WINTER
SPARE TIRE ALE

...AND AFTER.
HEY... IT'S GOTTA GO SOMEWHERE.
ANYBODY GOT AN ADVIL?
OLD GUYS WHO GET FAT IN WINTER
© OSGRAD '96 MAD DOG MEDIA

10-7-96 DuPont's Lycra Power: Think of it as a compression sack for that sleeping bag you're wearing around your waistline.

CROSS-TRAINING: ONE SIZE DOES NOT FIT ALL.
WELL, THEY SAID SNOWSHOEING IS AN EXCELLENT OFF-SEASON WORKOUT...
ESPECIALLY IF YOU'RE BEING CHASED BY A GILA MONSTER.
... HE'S GAINING ON YA, BY THE WAY.
OLD GUYS WHO GET FAT IN WINTER
©O'GRADY '97 MAD DOG MEDIA

1-13-97 Don't you hate those one-size-fits-all training stories spotlighting activities you could do if only you lived somewhere else?

WELLSIR, YOUR DISH IS OK...
... AND THE TEEVEE CHECKS OUT, TOO. I'D SAY WHAT YOU'RE SEEING REALLY IS THAT TOOR DOO FRANCE THING...
CRASH BANG SHRIEK BLIMEY, ADRIAN, WE'VE ANOTHER PILEUP...
SHOOT, NOBODY TOLD ME THEY WERE LETTING CAT. 5's IN... MAYBE NEXT YEAR...
BOB'S TV REPAIR
OLD GUYS WHO GET FAT IN WINTER
SPARE TIRE ALE
FAT IN A SACK
©O'GRADY97 MAD DOG MEDIA

7-28-97 The 1997 Tour had more crashes than a Cat. V crit. Victims included Marco Pantani, Tony Rominger, Eugeni Berzin, Alex Zülle and Ivan Gotti. The Fat Guy couldn't believe it either.

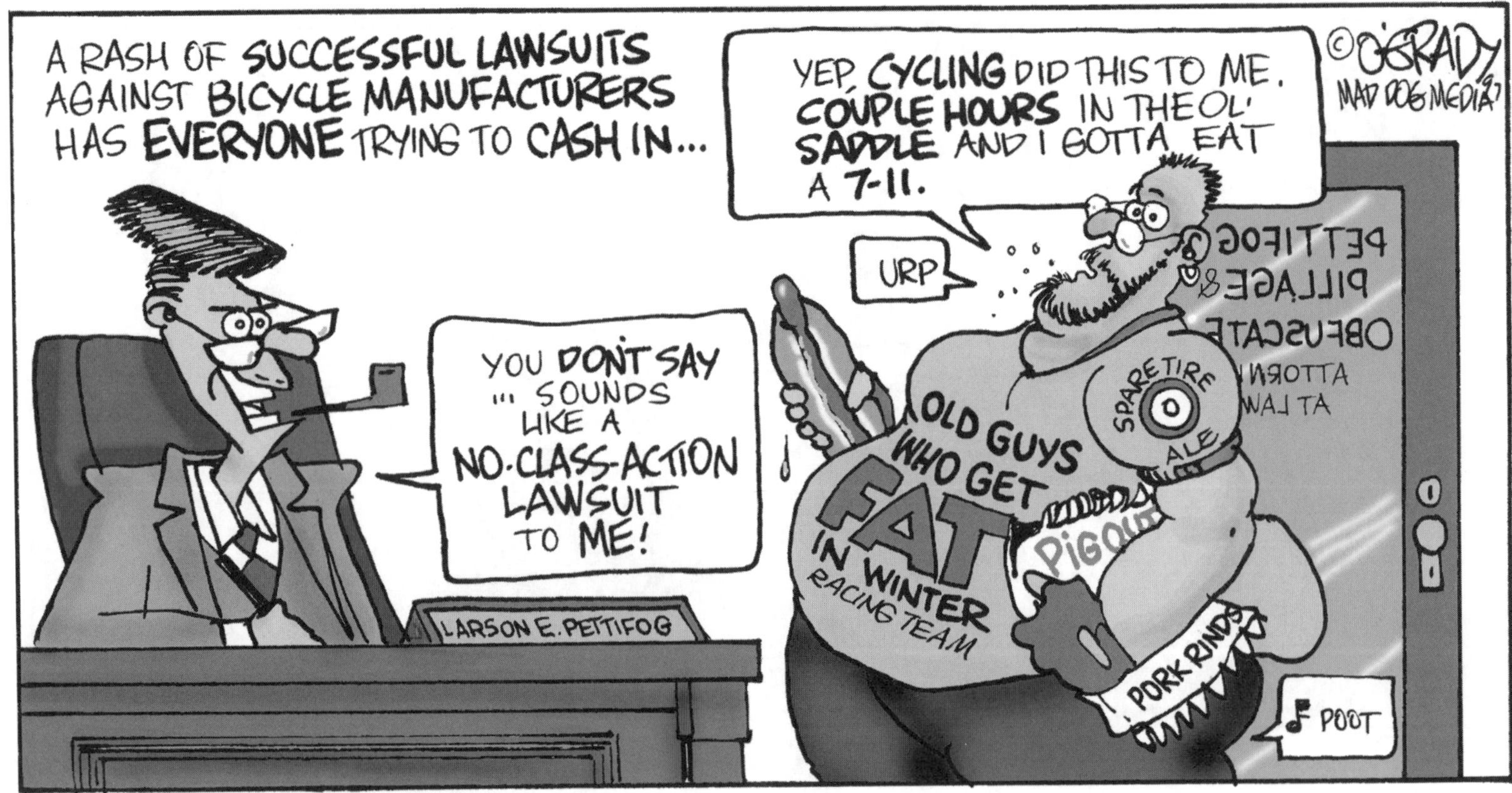
A RASH OF SUCCESSFUL LAWSUITS AGAINST BICYCLE MANUFACTURERS HAS EVERYONE TRYING TO CASH IN...
YEP, CYCLING DID THIS TO ME. COUPLE HOURS IN THE OL' SADDLE AND I GOTTA EAT A 7-11.
©O'GRADY MAD DOG MEDIA '97
URP
YOU DON'T SAY ... SOUNDS LIKE A NO-CLASS-ACTION LAWSUIT TO ME!
PETTIFOG PILLAGE & OBFUSCATE ATTORNEYS AT LAW
SPARE TIRE ALE
OLD GUYS WHO GET FAT IN WINTER RACING TEAM
LARSON E. PETTIFOG
PORK RINDS
POOT

9-1-97 "Bicycling is an inherently dangerous activity." It says so right there in the athlete's release form. Lawyers, the Fat Guy—and, in some mind-boggling cases, juries—were saying something completely different.

MEANWHILE, ON THE BMX CIRCUIT...
© O'GRADY 97
MAD DOG MEDIA
WHOOPS
THAT'S WHAT I CALL "BIG" AIR...
I WISH THIS OL' DUDE WOULD GO BACK TO @#!!!*! CYCLO-CROSS...
I'M TIRED OF ALL THEM CALLS FROM NORAD AND THE NATIONAL EARTHQUAKE CENTER.
MR. MOTO'S HOUSE O' HAM
SPARE TIRE ALE
OLD GUYS WHO GET FAT IN WINTER
LARDACHE
BMX WEAR FOR BIG GUYS
13

10-27-97 BMX was the next "big" thing as 1997 came to a close.

OFF-SEASON TRAINING (EL NIÑO STYLE)...
LOOKS LIKE MORE SNOW, RAIN, WIND, TORNADOES, TSUNAMIS, EARTHQUAKES, MUDSLIDES, FLASH FLOODS, PLAGUES OF LOCUSTS, NIGHTS OF THE LIVING DEAD...
CHANNEL-CHANGER REPEATS BETWEEN THE WEATHER CHANNEL (THE GROUNDHOG EXPLODED) AND OUTDOOR LIFE (NO CYCLING, LOTSA FISHING)
CLICK CLICK CLICK
@#!!!★@!?!!!
LACTATE THRESHOLD CURSING
©O'GRADY98
MAD DOG MEDIA
FLUID REPLACEMENT
MORE FLUID REPLACEMENT
SPARE TIRE ALE
OLD GUYS WHO GET FAT IN WINTER
SPARE TIRE STOUT
SPARE TIRE PORTER
SPARE TIRE AMBER
SPARE TIRE LITE
POWER CLENCHING

3-16-98 In Colorado, March and spring have absolutely nothing in common, especially when that Al Niño dude is out and about.

© O'GRADY '98
MAD DOG MEDIA
THANKS TO CHARLES PELKEY
WE DON'T ORDINARILY DO THIS, JAN... BUT YOUR EXAMPLE HAS BEEN SO INSPIRING THAT WE WAIVED THE AGE RESTRICTIONS...
UH HUH... ZO, YOU GONNA EAT ZOSE FRIES?
GOD, IT JUST MAKES ME FEEL SO ... HUNGRY.
CLAP
CLAP
CLAP
SNIF
JUMBO PRETZELS
OLD GUYS WHO GET FAT IN WINTER RACING TEAM
XXXL
BUCKET O' BRATS
SPARE TIRE ALE
WINTER

4-27-98 How fat was Jan Ullrich? His shadow weighed 180. When he had to haul ass, it took two trips. Why, he was so fat, he finished second in the Tour. Badaboom, badabing.

THE ANNUAL PILGRIMAGE TO THE SHRINE OF ST. PHIL BEGINS...
WELCOME TO OUR COVERAGE OF THE 1998 TOUR DE FRANCE!
HELLO, MABEL? MADGE HERE. WHADDAYA SAY TO A LITTLE THREE-WEEK VACATION? NO... ANYWHERE BUT FRANCE.
GIVE US THIS DAY OUR DAILY STAGE AND FORGIVE US OUR CHANNEL-SURFING DURING THE @#!!! COMMERCIALS...
OLD GEEZERS WHO FAT WIN IN RACIN
WIDE LOAD DINER
SPARETIRE ALE
© O'GRADY '98
MAD DOG MEDIA

7-28-98 Our Phil, who art in Heaven, hallowed be Thy name. That Karsten dude has to go, though. Amen.

DUDE, NO MATTER HOW MANY RINGS YOU GROW, NOONE IS GONNA MISTAKE YOU FOR A SATURN RACER.
YOU THINK THIS IS WEIRD? I USED TO HAVE A BUNCH OF SMALLER RIDERS ORBITING AROUND ME...
CRUNCH
MUNCH
MUNCH
SPARE TIRE ALE
OLD GUYS WHO GET FAT IN WINTER RACING TEAM
FEED BAG DINER
MACK
CREAK
PING
SQUEAK
ROAD TOADZ
©O'GRADY '99
MAD DOG MEDIA

2-8-99 Saturn seemed to be sponsoring everything in 1999. If they only made a four-wheel-drive truck....

THE FAT'S IN THE FIRE AT CACTUS CUP...
YEAH, I'DA PROBABLY WON IF ALL THE LUGS ON MY FRAME HADN'T BROKEN FOR SOME REASON WHEN I DROPPED OFF "THE LEDGE."
IT REMINDS ME OF THAT TIME NED, TOMES AND I WERE SHREDDIN' AT PURGATORY IN '91... BABBLE YAMMER JABBER
DUDE CASTS THE ONLY SHADE IN THE PARK, BUT THESE BLASTS OF HOT AIR ARE KILLIN' ME.
SPARE TIRE ALE
OLD GUYS WHO GET FAT IN WINTER
WHITE THIGHS VELO
© O'GRADY '99
MAD DOG MEDIA

4-5-99 To my knowledge, this was my first Cactus Cup gag that didn't turn someone into a pincushion.

Stuffed Shirts

Emperors, New Clothes and Fashion Critics

HONEY, QUIT FIDDLING WITH THOSE AWARDS AND GO RIDE YOUR BIKE, FOR GODSAKES!
YOU'RE SCARING THE DOG, AND YOUR OFFICE SMELLS FUNNY.
MUTTER MUMBLE...
WHY EVERYTHING SUCKS BY PATRICK O'GRADY
MAD DOG MEDIA
DRAW INCREDIBLY FUNNY CARTOON HERE X
VENOM
ENEMIES LIST
THINGS TO DO 1. SLAM FEDS 2. SEE 1.
LIES LIES LIES
ACID
THE ANARCHIST COOKBOOK
©O'GRADY '98 MAD DOG MEDIA

I have this problem with authority; I can neither wield it nor yield to it, so whenever I encounter it, I stick my thumbs in my ears, waggle my fingers and go like this: "*Ppppppffffffbbbbblllllll!*"

It's nothing personal. But if you're over there doing that, I'm probably going to be over here doing this. Dad pulled a 30-year hitch in the Blue Zoomies, voted the straight GOP ticket and drank 12-ounce martinis; I grew my hair down to my sandals, joined a Communist party and sold whatever dope I wasn't using at the time. It seemed the thing to do. Although if I'd known then that my head contained a finite amount of hair, I wouldn't have let it all out before I turned 30.

This unnatural contrariness is why I work at home. Several former employers and all my current ones have insisted upon it. This is also why I write and draw unkind things about USA Cycling, the Union Cycliste Internationale, and the other overinflated windbags that float over our sport, kept aloft by hot air generated through their burning of our money.

It's not so much that the scum has floated to the top of these stagnant, bureaucratic ponds is so hideously repellent, so intolerably foul, so choking an effluent that it impedes the free flow of our sport. It's just that I can't see a pond without peeing into it.

Some people don't think that's funny. Most of them live in one of these ponds. Others look down their noses and sniff, "As if these ponds weren't polluted enough already."

Me, I keep hoping that my periodic contributions of a little acid will help dissolve the clog and flush the offending blockage away. Mostly, it doesn't. But sometimes I hear giggles from people riding past the cesspool.

Ppppppffffffbbbbbllllll!

©O'GRADY '93
MAD DOG MEDIA
THANKS TO SHANNON
DUDE, I MUST HAVE THE WORST CASE OF THE BONK ANYONE'S EVER HEARD OF ... I COULDA SWORN I JUST SAW A GUY IN A THREE-PIECE SUIT AND A BALLET SKIRT FIGURESKATING INTO THE SUNSET...
NAWW... THAT'S JUST JERRY LACE.
Patrick O'Grady cartoon

5-10-93 Executive director Jerry Lace leaves USCF for the U.S. Figure Skating Association.

OHH... HINCAPIE DISPUTED MY CALL, AND I SAID, "TOUGH." THEN HE SAID HE COULD FIX IT SO MY HEAD REALLY WAS WHERE IT APPEARED TO BE, AND I SAID, "OH YEAH?" AND ONE THING LED TO ANOTHER...
FINISH
DON'T WORRY... I SAW THE WHOLE THING.
GRRRR...
TAP TAPPITY TAP TAP
©O'GRADY '93
MAD DOG MEDIA
Patrick O'Grady cartoon

5-31-93 George Hincapie was stripped of the win in stage eight of the Tour DuPont. "This is bullshit," said surrogate winner Dave Rayner. "Indeed it was," wrote VN editor John Wilcockson.

ANOTHER NEW BIKE EH, GRAEME?
OH, SHUT UP AND FETCH ME A SPANNER...
... AND SOME BAND-AIDS...
TINK
CLANK
PING
DONG
WHANK

1-13-95 Graeme Obree wasn't much luckier. He kept breaking tradition and records, and the UCI kept breaking his balls.

RECENT SUCCESSES AT WORLD'S ENCOURAGE A NEW LINE OF RESEARCH AT USCF SPORTS SCIENCE...
I DON'T CARE HOW MANY @#!!!☆@! RAINBOW JERSEYS NOTHSTEIN WON! YOU'RE NOT BREAKING MY @#!!!★?! FEET!!
WHAT CAN I TELL YA? IT WORKS...
WE'LL GET YOU A NICE CARBON-FIBER CRUTCH...
GRUNT
STRUGGLE
THRASH
USA
PARK

9-12-94 Marty Nothstein won gold in the men's sprint and keirin at the 1994 track world's while recovering from a broken foot. The next step seemed obvious, and if that step required crutches, well ... you can't make an omelet without breaking bones.

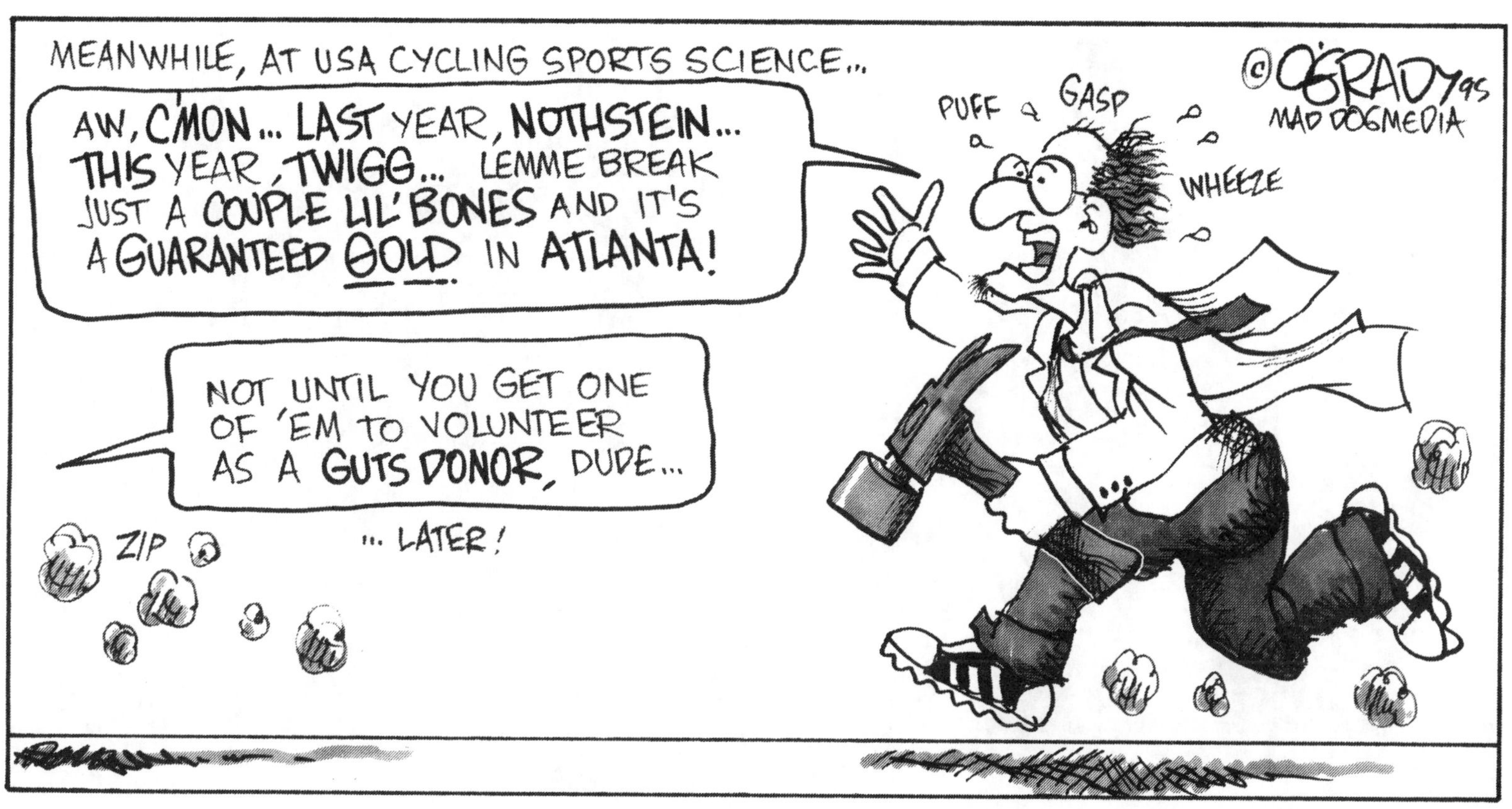
MEANWHILE, AT USA CYCLING SPORTS SCIENCE...
©O'GRADY95 MAD DOGMEDIA
AW, C'MON... LAST YEAR, NOTHSTEIN... THIS YEAR, TWIGG... LEMME BREAK JUST A COUPLE LIL' BONES AND IT'S A GUARANTEED GOLD IN ATLANTA!
PUFF
GASP
WHEEZE
NOT UNTIL YOU GET ONE OF 'EM TO VOLUNTEER AS A GUTS DONOR, DUDE...
ZIP
... LATER!

8-23-95 Those guys in the lab really know how to put the hammer down. This time the inspiration was Rebecca Twigg, kicking butt with a pinned collarbone.

GASP
WHEEZE
HORK
CHOKE
THEY KEEP SAYING THEY'RE BEHIND ME ... AND I'VE FELT THEM THERE MANY, MANY TIMES. NNNGGGHHHH...
PICK IT UP, SON... I GOTTA MEETING...
BEEP
...JP! HOW THE HELL ARE YA? NOW, ABOUT THIS SPONSORSHIP DEAL...
...OF COURSE WE'RE TALKING ELITE PROGRAM HERE...
LICENSEES
USA CYCLING INC.
NO RIDERS
©O'GRADY '95
MAD DOG MEDIA

10-8-95 Some folks—including a horrified Inside Communications executive, now departed—thought the passenger looked like USCF managing director Steve Penny. I didn't think he looked like anyone; I was having trouble making the adjustment to cartooning in color.

LOOKS A LOT BIGGER THE CLOSER HE GETS, HUH?
DUUUUUDE...
RRRRR...
©O'GRADY '96 MAD DOG MEDIA
ATLANTA OLYMPICS
USCF
NORBA

2-26-96 This guy I knew. Scooter Trash was a character I'd used in editorial cartoons to portray government and other evildoers.

WHAT THE HELL IS IT?
WELL, IT AIN'T @#!!! BARNEY, DUDE...
RRRR...
©O'GRADY '96 MAD DOG MEDIA
Shaklee
Sha

7-1-96 Revenge of the Bostisaurus: Three times an alternate, 42-year-old Kent Bostick made the Olympic team in the 4000-meter pursuit.

MEANWHILE, AT THE OLYMPICS...
C'MAN, C'MAAAN... PUDDEM UP, PUDDEM UPP... I'LL MURDELIZE YA, YA BUM... HUFF PUFF
LEAP CAVORT DANCE SHUFFLE
WHAT A RELIEF...
...I VAS AFRAID ZEY WOULD SEND TOMAC!
AWW, I THINK HE'S KINDA CUTE...
EUROS
MTB
LIVE TO RIDE RIDE TO LIVE
GOLD
FEAR THIS
GRUNDIG ÜBER ALLES
© O'GRADY '96 MAD DOG MEDIA

7-15-96 John Tomac did not make that Olympic team, despite leading the Jeep National Championship Series as the Games approached.

THE GOOD NEWS IS YOU ONLY HAVE TO EAT IT ONCE EVERY FOUR YEARS...
USA CYCLING
BORN TO LOSE
TODAY'S SPECIAL ATLANTA ON A SHINGLE
GO USA
WIN GOLD
© O'GRADY '96 MAD DOG MEDIA

8-19-96 The Atlanta Olympic Games were more of a soup kitchen than a banquet.

I KEEP TELLING YOU... SURE, YOUR POSITION IS LEGAL...
... BUT YOU GOTTA HAVE A BIKE!
HEY... THIS IS HOW WE DO IT ON KRYPTON, DUDE...
UCI
© O'GRADY '96 MAD DOG MEDIA

9-23-96 The Clark Kents at the UCI declare the "Superman" position legal.

HORRORS! WHY, THIS HIGH-TECH BIKE APPEARS TO IMPERIL THE SACRED IDEAL OF MANO-A-MANO COMPETITION!
GEE... YOU DON'T SAY.
IMAGINE MY DISMAY...
DOPE
ëuros
BETTER CYCLING THROUGH CHEMISTRY
UCI
© O'GRADY '96
MAD DOG MEDIA

11-18-96 The UCI gets tough on superbikes in search of a level playing field. There is no masking agent for juiced-up bikes.

IT DIDN'T BEAR ANY FRUIT THIS SUMMER... THINK IT NEEDS PRUNING?
WELL, IF I DID, I SURE AS HELL WOULDN'T TELL YOU, CITY BOY.
TWIGG
USA CYCLING
VELO NEWS
USA CYCLING NURSERY
©O'GRADY '96 MAD DOG MEDIA

12-16-96 Rebecca Twigg and USA Cycling cut a deal before a disciplinary hearing stemming from her abrupt departure from the '96 Olympic team. The plea bargain included a confidentiality agreement.

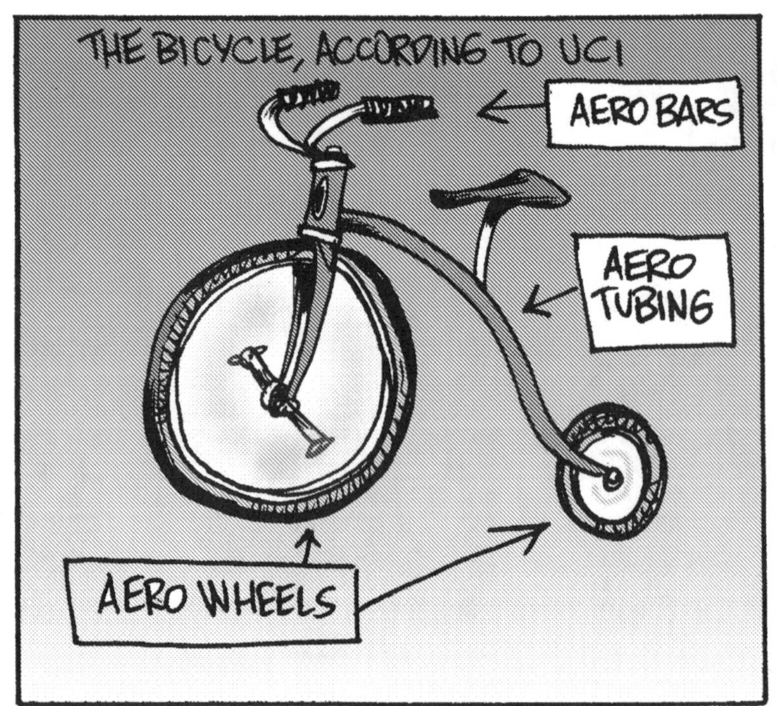

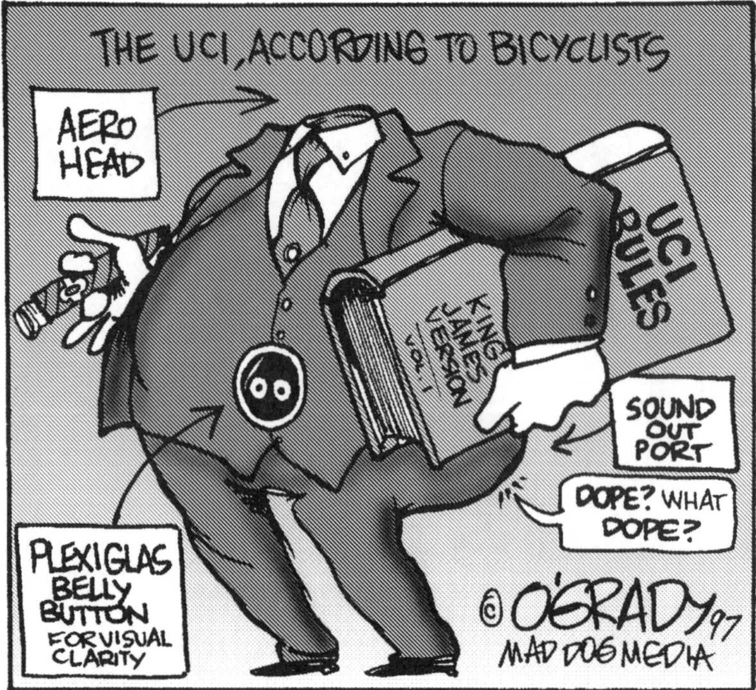

2-24-97 It's hard to tell who has the worse case of cranial-anal impaction: the see-no-evil UCI ...

A VENGEFUL SOFTWARE ENGINEER-CYCLIST DESIGNS AN INTERACTIVE APPLICATION SPECIFICALLY FOR HIS TORMENTORS ON REC. BICYCLES. RACING.
FLAME OUT TM
PEE SEA
WANK R TANK SELF LOVE LUBE
© O'GRADY '97 MAD DOG MEDIA

3-17-97 ... or the venomous denizens haunting the Usenet newsgroup rec.bicycles.racing.

THE UCI TECHNICAL COMMITTEE HANDS DOWN ANOTHER FAR-SIGHTED DECISION FOR THE GOOD OF THE SPORT...
OOK OOK OOK...
NEW BIKE
AERO
bike
Good
© O'GRADY MAD DOG MEDIA '97

4-28-97 The UCI is not so much Luddite as preindustrial.

I'M SHOCKED! SHOCKED! TO LEARN THAT BLOOD DOPING MAY BE OCCURRING IN THIS SPORT!
TAKE TWO WEEKS OFF.
THE DEVIL YOU SAY.
UCI
SUSPENSION!
DEAR CLAUDIO, YOU HAVE TOO MUCH BLOOD IN YOUR BLOOD. LOVE, UCI
IL DIABLO
666
©O'GRADY 97 MAD DOG MEDIA

5-26-97 Claudio "Il Diablo" Chiappucci draws a suspension for having too much blood in his blood.

WHADDAYA MEAN, THERE'S NOBODY LEFT?
WHO'S GONNA SEND OUT TH' MEMBERSHIP RENEWALS? PUT OUT TH' MAGAZINES? FIND ME A NEW AX SPONSOR?
Y'KNOW, THIS MAY NOT DO MUCH FOR MY RÉSUMÉ, BUT IT'S DONE WONDERS FOR THAT NAGGING PAIN IN MY ASS.
USA CYCLING
©O'GRADY '97
MAD DOG MEDIA

9-27-97 The traditional post-Olympics sackings and resignations continued apace ...

FREEZE! UCI!
HANDS BEHIND YOUR HEAD!
CRASH!
HILLS
SPRINTS
VELO HYPO
OK, YOU GOT ME... I GUESS I'M IN SOME BIG TROUBLE, HUH?
WHAT, YOU WORRIED ABOUT ALL THAT DOPE? NAW, WE'RE LOOKING FOR AERO' GEAR!
PLACE IS CLEAN, BOSS ... JUST A LITTLE EPO, COKE, METH, 'ROIDS ...
©O'GRADY98 MAD DOG MEDIA
THANKS TO GILBERT SHELTON

2-23-98 ... as did the UCI's fascination with aero' gear. This cartoon was inspired by two Freak Brothers drug-bust classics.

OKAY! OKAY! HOW ABOUT THESE? CAN I RACE WITH THESE HANDLEBARS?
BUT OF COURSE... PROVIDING YOU PUT UP THREE MONTHS' WAGES FOR TWO YEARS, HAVE TEN RIDERS, OBTAIN OUR APPROVAL FOR THEIR CONTRACTS AND YOUR BUDGET, SHAVE YOUR LEGS WITH A UCI-APPROVED RAZOR, DRINK ONLY WARM BEER, WEAR LEDERHOSEN, DRIVE ON THE LEFT SIDE OF ALL ROADS, REFRAIN FROM SHOWERING, ADOPT THE METRIC SYSTEM...
©O'GRADY '98 MAD DOG MEDIA
THE BIG BOOK OF RULES
LITTLE BITTY U.S. TEAMS
UCI
1) APPROACH
2) KNEEL
3) SPEAK WHEN SPOKEN TO

4-13-98 *The Big Book of Rules* just keeps getting bigger.

©O'GRADY 98
MAD DOG MEDIA
YOU ARE CORDIALLY INVITED TO APPLY FOR ANOTHER POSITION WITH THE CREW...
OBOY.
DIST. REPS
HMS USA CYCLING
PUNT
I FEEL SO... EMPOWERED.

5-28-98 Meanwhile, USA Cycling planned to replace USCF's district-rep network with a scattering of regional reps.

NEWS ITEM: USA CYCLING PLANS TO BUILD UPON THE "SUCCESS" OF PROJECT '96...
"PROJECT TRIAD?"
... MAYBE IT'S A THREE-SEATER.
• PROJECT '96 •
COMING SOON: PROJECT TRIAD!
USA
© O'GRADY '98 MAD DOG MEDIA

7-13-98 You can find your membership dollars inside, under the lid.

CYCLING'S BIGGEST DOPE PROBLEM ...HEIN VERBRUGGEN.
WE HAVE AN EFFECTIVE DOPING-CONTROL PROGRAM...
... NOW, IF YOU'LL EXCUSE ME, I HAVE A PLANE TO CATCH...
INDIA
CUBA
©O'GRADY 98 MAD DOG MEDIA

8-31-98 Across the pond, Le Tour was awash in a drug scandal so severe that it threatened to imperil UCI honcho Hein Verbruggen's vacation. Or not.

11-16-98 USA Cycling started unloading the district reps.

Everybody Else

BLOODY FOINE WEATHER F'A CYCLE RACE, EH, SEAN?
RIGHTO, DAVID
OOO... PARIS-ROUBAIX.
SPARE TIRE STOUT
OLD GUYS WHO STAY FAT YEAR-ROU
ROOT ROOT
AMAZING GREASE BURGERS
©OGRADY '97 MAD DOG MEDIA

"Stop them damn pictures!"

Mad dogs will bite the hand that feeds them, and that's basically what I've been doing for a decade. How have I remained at large for so long, chasing my betters on their bicycles? Why has no one had me put to sleep, or at least neutered? Beats me.

In being allowed to comment on cycling in *VeloNews*, I have been elevated well above my station. I have neither the encyclopedic knowledge of editor John Wilcockson nor the cycling résumé of Bob Roll. I don't draw nearly as well as David Brinton, and I lack the sensitivity of Maynard Hershon.

But I have that little knowledge which is a dangerous thing, I race now and again, and when sober I can scribble something that kind of looks like a fat guy on a bike. As for sensitivity, well...we'll leave that to my man Maynard. Because a cartoonist should have all the sensitivity of a sandpaper condom.

"Stop them damn pictures," bellowed Boss Tweed, skewered by the pen of *Harper's Weekly* caricaturist Thomas Nast. "I don't care a straw for your newspaper articles. My constituents can't read. But they can't help seeing them damn pictures!"

Them damn pictures. Mine aren't a patch on Nast's, which brought down Tammany Hall. Nor are they equal to the art of Pat Oliphant or Jeff MacNelly, the sharpest edi-

MEANWHILE, AT PARIS-ROUBAIX...
WOW, MAN, WHAT HAPPENED TO YOU?
AW, FOUR GUYS FROM MAPEI PASSED ME SO FAST I THOUGHT MY BIKE HAD STOPPED...
... SO I GOT OFF TO SEE WHAT WAS THE MATTER.
©O'GRADY'96 MAD DOG MEDIA
APOLOGIES TO GILBERT S.
GS
OTB

A tribute to underground cartoonist Gilbert Shelton.

torial cartoonists of the modern era. I met Oliphant once, and he was gracious enough to pass on some tips, which is like having Sean Kelly tell you how to ride a spring classic.

Frankly, my approach owes less to Nast than to Gilbert Shelton's Fabulous Furry Freak Brothers (Shelton drew one of the funniest bike cartoons ever in 1971, and I paid homage to it a quarter-century later in a cartoon about Mapei going one-two-three at Paris-Roubaix). I'm more interested in comedy than crusades. While the bellowing of an skewered big shot is enjoyable, it's laughter that's music to my ears.

Cycling has more than its share of serious journalists. Me, I'm just another wise-cracking spectator craning his neck over the course tape, bitching about how the feds are screwing everything up, grumbling about who's on the juice, and trying to catch a glimpse of Lance Armstrong or Alison Dunlap as they charge by, larger than life and twice as fast.

The only difference between me and you is I get paid for it.

4-14-89 Critics likened the nebulous National Cycle League to Gertrude Stein's Oakland, saying there was no there there.

4-28-89 Good races kept disappearing back then, too.

... AND SO IN THIS TOUR DE FRANCE WE'VE SHOWN YOU THE LOUVRE, THE EIFFEL TOWER, THE JUSTLY FAMED BORDEAUX WINE COUNTRY AND A 118-YEAR-OLD MAN WITH A PICTURE OF BERNARD HINAULT TATTOOED ON HIS LEFT BUTTOCK. THE TOUR TRULY IS A SPECTACLE — AND DON'T WE WISH WE KNEW WHERE IT IS.
CINZANO
ANO
abc
©O'GRADY 89
VELONEWS
Patrick O'Grady cartoon

5-12-89 Sunflowers, schmunflowers...where the hell's the race?

WELL, SO MUCH FOR THE OLD SPEEDING BULLET...
©O'GRADY
VELONEWS
KAPOW!
PEEYOW!
ZING!
7 ELEVEn
Coors LIGHT
THUD
Patrick O'Grady cartoon

5-26-89 7-Eleven waxed the Coors Light-ADR team—including 27th-placed Greg LeMond—in the inaugural Tour de Trump.

HOW THE FINAL TIME-TRIAL COURSE
IN THE TOUR DE TRUMP WAS DESIGNED...
© O'GRADY/89
VELONEWS
THAT'S IT!
GOO?
TOUR
de
TRUMP
MAP

6-16-89 That final TT had more twists than a Quentin Tarantino script. Eric Vanderaerden lost his way…and the race.

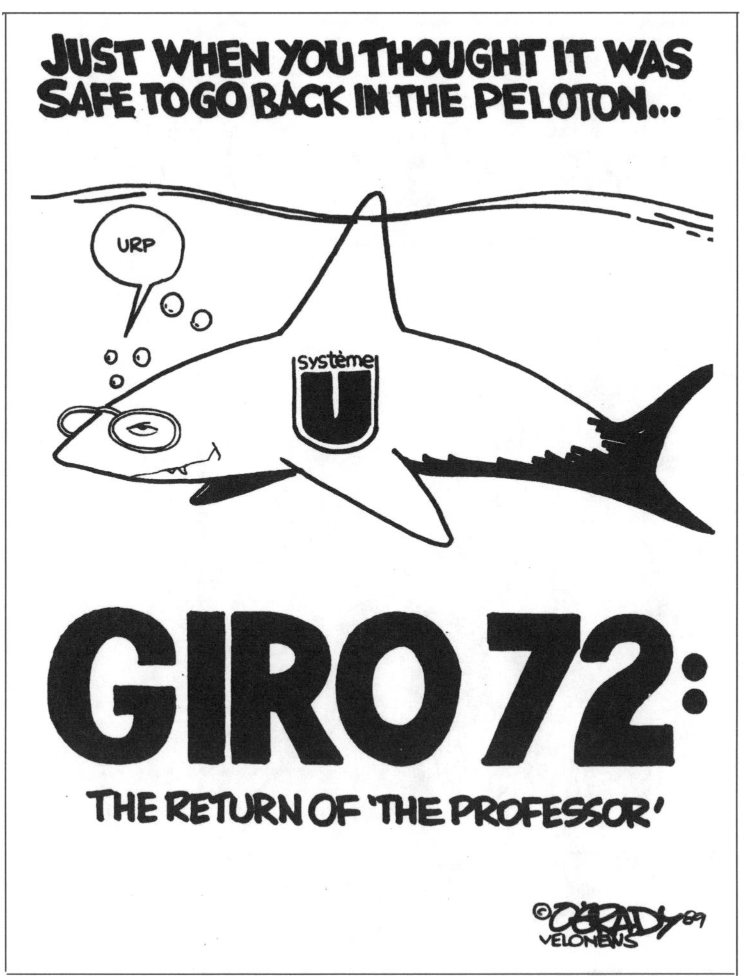
JUST WHEN YOU THOUGHT IT WAS SAFE TO GO BACK IN THE PELOTON...
URP
système
U
GIRO 72:
THE RETURN OF 'THE PROFESSOR'
©O'GRADY '89
VELONEWS

6-30-89 Laurent Fignon gobbled up the Giro and wanted the Tour for dessert.

THE OFFICIAL
TOUR® WINNERS WATCH!
KEEP TRACK OF TIME LIKE A PRO!
TEARDROP RESISTANT
TILT
KISS IT GOODBYE
WIN
LOSE
HEY STUPID! YOU MISSED YOUR START TIME!
AHHHAHAHA
PROGRAMMABLE ALARM AVAILABLE NOW IN SPANISH AND WORDS OF ONE SYLLABLE (EXTRA)
ENDORSED BY THE CATEGORY IV HELMETLESS CRASH SURVIVORS ASSN.
©O'GRADY '89
VELONEWS
Patrick O'Grady cartoon

7-14-89 Speaking of eating it, defending Tour champion Pedro Delgado started the prologue 2:40 late and lost more than seven minutes in the first two days.

I DON'T GET IT... ONE MINUTE I'M SHOVELING IN THE DIRT...
THE NEXT, I'M FLAT ON MY BACK AND MY SHIRT IS GONE!
GREG LEMOND
HE DIED IN THE ALPS 1989
©O'GRADY '89 VELONEWS
Patrick O'Grady cartoon

9-8-89 The Professor must've flunked aerodynamics. He rode bareheaded, without aero' bars, in the '89 Tour's final time trial, and lost to Greg LeMond by 8 seconds.

THE
WOMAN RACER
(AS SEEN BY PROMOTERS, SPONSORS AND THE USCF)
HONEY? DINNER'S READY...
WHY DON'T YOU SIT DOWN AND EAT WHILE I CLEAN YOUR CHAIN?
FUTURE TOUR DE FRA LEADER
GERBER
Patrick O'Grady cartoon
© O'GRADY '89 VELONEWS

1-29-90 This one pissed off a lot of people who shot right past the parenthetical qualification and went straight to the gratuitous sexism.

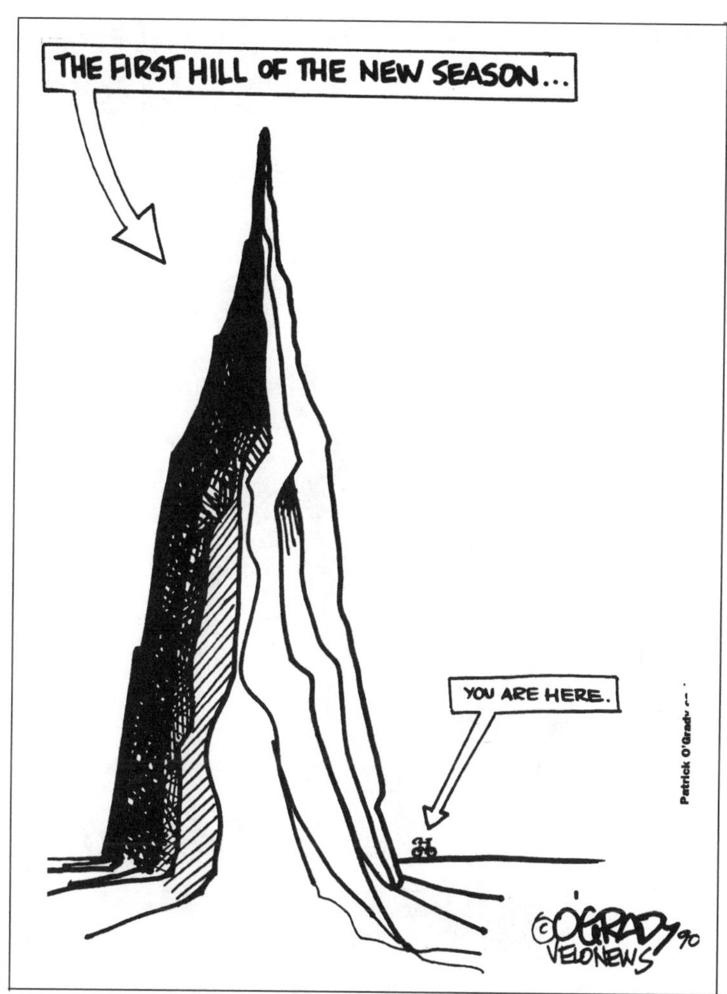
THE FIRST HILL OF THE NEW SEASON...
YOU ARE HERE.
© O'GRADY '90 VELONEWS

2-19-90 This one didn't bother anyone.

UM... I'LL HAVE A BEER IF IT'S ALL THE SAME TO YOU.
VELO FASTO
PERRIER-BENZENE CUP
FASTO
THIS END UP
Patrick O'Grady cartoon
© O'GRADY 90 VELONEWS

3-12-90 Perrier was sponsoring the World Cup. It also was having a little trouble with benzene contamination.

NOT TO WORRY, FOLKS... ONLY A FLESH WOUND...
... AND YOU BE SURE TO KEEP THOSE CARDS AND LETTERS COMING IN.
ANYBODY GOT ANY BACTINE?
LETTERS
O'G
HIDEOUSLY TASTELESS CARTOONS FOR FUN & PROFIT
VENOM
O'GRADY
Patrick O'Grady cartoon
© O'GRADY 90 VELONEWS

3-26-90 He who lives by the pen shall die by the pen.

JUNIOR RACER "QUADS" ZITOWSKI FINALLY GETS THAT 86 RING HE'S BEEN DREAMING OF...
VIDEO TO GO
ATOMIC SOUND
©O'GRADY '90
VELONEWS
Patrick O'Grady cartoon

4-9-90 Gear restrictions for juniors? Bah. Let 'em blow out their knees like the rest of us.

... SO THIS GUY CALLS TO ASK IF WE'RE COVERING THE TOUR OF TEXAS AND I SEZ, 'GUYS WITH SHAVED LEGS WEARIN' PANTY HOSE AND RIDIN' BIKES? THAT AIN'T NO SPORT! WHERE'S THE BLOOD?'
FUNNY YOU SHOULD ASK.
UH... CHARLEY...
BOB'S GUN SHOPPE
FINAL DAZE KARATE
ROAD KILL VELO
666
SPORTS
~OUR MOTTO~ IF IT'S GOT A BALL WE PRINT IT ALL
©O'GRADY '90 VELONEWS
Patrick O'Grady cartoon

4-23-90 The mainstream press: Give 'em a ball and they'll follow you anywhere.

CRITERIUM ETIQUETTE
8
ALWAYS APOLOGIZE AFTER WALKING ACROSS THE COURSE DURING A FIELD SPRINT.
I BEG YOUR PARDON... YOU WASN'T WINNIN' OR NOTHIN', WAS YA?
MMMFFUUGGLL... *
BUBBA BAR
GRÜNT
13
©O'GRADY '90 VELONEWS
*NO, IT'S QUITE ALL RIGHT. THANKS.
Patrick O'Grady cartoon

5-7-90 Hit them boogers. They're a lot softer than asphalt.

WILD BILL PAPADAPOLOUS:
CORNER MARSHAL
AH DONE TOLD HIM NOT TO CROSS NO STREET DURIN' NO FIEL' SPRINT.
USCF
©O'GRADY '90 VELONEWS
Patrick O'Grady cartoon

5-28-90 Here in Colorado, of course, we just shoot 'em.

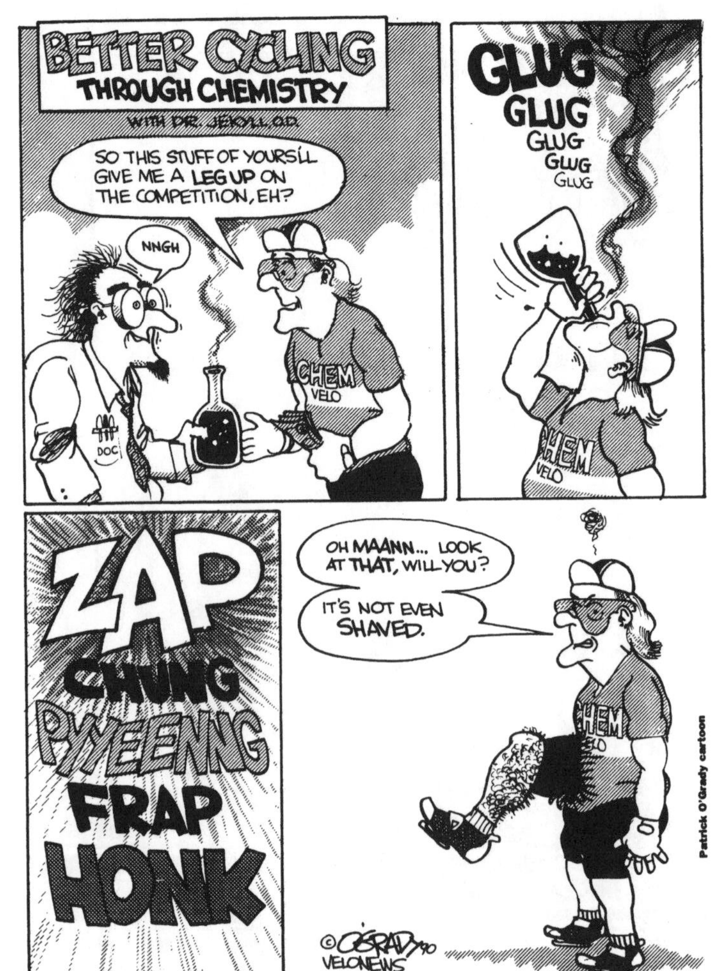
BETTER CYCLING
THROUGH CHEMISTRY
WITH DR. JEKYLL O.D.
SO THIS STUFF OF YOURS'LL GIVE ME A LEG UP ON THE COMPETITION, EH?
NNGH
CHEM VELO
DOC
GLUG
GLUG
GLUG
GLUG
GLUG
ZAP
CHUNG
PYYEENNG
FRAP
HONK
OH MAANN... LOOK AT THAT, WILL YOU?
IT'S NOT EVEN SHAVED.
©O'GRADY '90
VELONEWS
Patrick O'Grady cartoon

6-25-90 You just can't make some people happy.

AND MEANWHILE, AT CORESTATES...
GRRR
CHEESEHEAD
SNARL
SLURPEE
'SCUSA ME.
7-ELEVEN
COORS LIGHT
GIS
BENOTTO
O'GRADY
VELONEWS
Patrick O'Grady cartoon

7-9-90 Household name Paolo Cimini won CoreStates after 7-Eleven and Coors Light beat each other into linguine.

JEEZ, MAN, WHAT HAPPENED TO YOU?
I DUNNO... LAST THING I REMEMBER IS DRINKING FROM THEUNISSE'S WATER BOTTLE...
HEY- GOT ANY WORMS ON YOU?
YOUR NAME HERE
THIS SPACE FOR RENT VELO
S SPACE R RENT VELO
©O'GRADY'90 VELONEWS
Patrick O'Grady cartoon

7-23-90 Come to think of it, Gert-Jan Theunisse always did fly up those hills.

PRAISE BE! HALLELUJAH! YEA, THOUGH HE RODE THROUGH THE VALLEY OF THE SHADOW OF...
BEHOLD HE IS RISEN
JESUS FREAK?
LEMOND FAN.
GREG
HOON
PDM
©O'GRADY'90 VELONEWS
Patrick O'Grady cartoon

8-6-90 Greg wins his third Tour. Praise him with great praise.

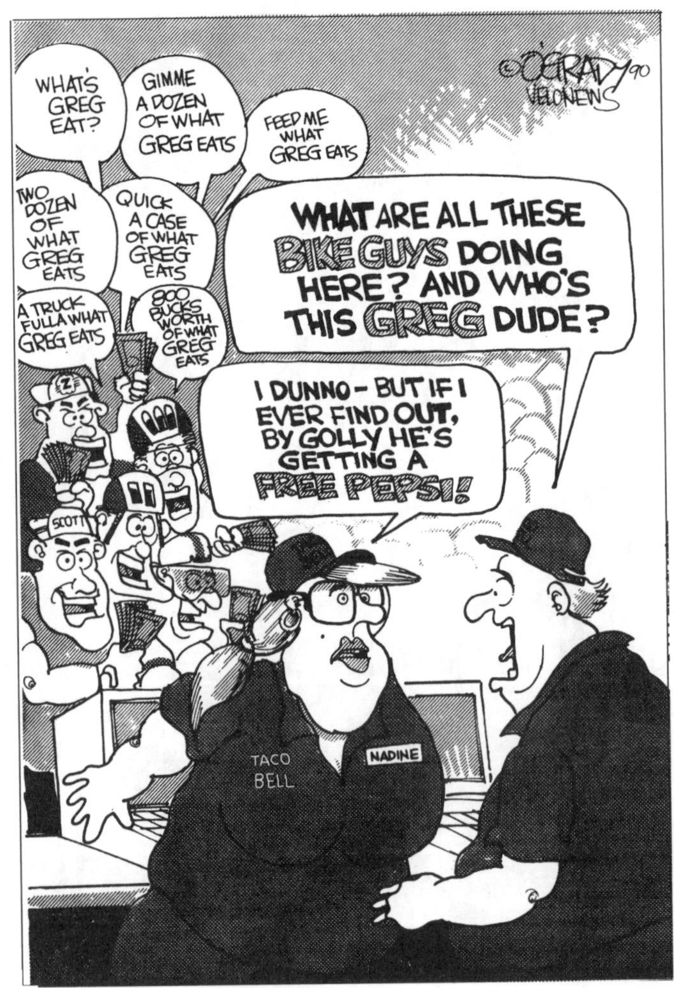
©O'GRADY '90 VELONEWS
WHAT'S GREG EAT?
GIMME A DOZEN OF WHAT GREG EATS
FEED ME WHAT GREG EATS
TWO DOZEN OF WHAT GREG EATS
QUICK A CASE OF WHAT GREG EATS
A TRUCK FULLA WHAT GREG EATS
800 BUCKS WORTH OF WHAT GREG EATS
WHAT ARE ALL THESE BIKE GUYS DOING HERE? AND WHO'S THIS GREG DUDE?
I DUNNO - BUT IF I EVER FIND OUT, BY GOLLY HE'S GETTING A FREE PEPSI!
SCOTT
TACO BELL
NADINE

8-27-90 Hey, Bubba…win three Tours and they'll eat what you eat, too. Even if you're a Chihuahua.

©O'GRADY '90 VELONEWS
OH WOW, DUDE… LIKE YOU'RE TOTALLY SHREDDING MY BUCKS! Y'KNOW? *
DINERO PEAK OFF-ROAD RACE REGISTRATION
SHADDAP.
OH WOW DUDE VELO
ASK ABOUT OUR EASY CREDIT PLAN
SIT DOWN FIRST
YES! WE ACCEPT YOUR BIKE AS DOWN PAYMENT!
WHEN ACCOMPANIED WITH ARM & LEG
Patrick O'Grady cartoon
* I CONSIDER YOUR ENTRY FEE SOMEWHAT EXCESSIVE, SIR.

10-22-90 Extortionary race-entry fees are hardly a new development.

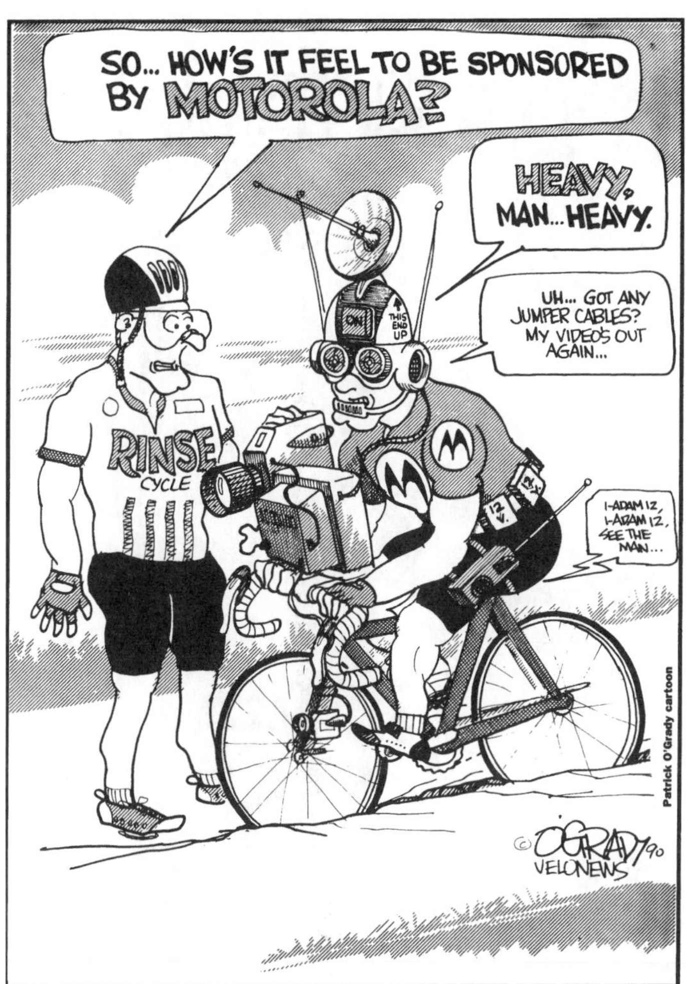
SO... HOW'S IT FEEL TO BE SPONSORED BY MOTOROLA?
HEAVY, MAN...HEAVY.
UH... GOT ANY JUMPER CABLES? MY VIDEO'S OUT AGAIN...
I-ADAM 12, I-ADAM 12, SEE THE MAN...
RINSE CYCLE
ON
THIS END UP
12 V.
©O'GRADY '90 VELONEWS
Patrick O'Grady cartoon

11-19-90 Breaker one-nine, you got the Motorola team. Got your ears on? Come back, good buddy.

SAY, YOU DON'T SUPPOSE THERE'S A TACO BELL IN THE NEIGHBORHOOD?
SHUT UP AND PEDAL, GREG...
©O'GRADY '91 VELONEWS
Patrick O'Grady cartoon

2-11-91 Greg was logging the big miles with support from a beefy motor home that made those cramped drive-up windows a little less accessible.

HHNNGKK!
HAAAAAACCCCKK
HHNNGKK!
HHNEEEEEGGH
NNK!
EEERRKKK
©O'GRADY '91 VELONEWS
THAT FIRST BIG HILL OF THE SEASON...
Patrick O'Grady cartoon

3-4-91 There's that hill again. Is it getting steeper, or am I just getting older? Don't answer that.

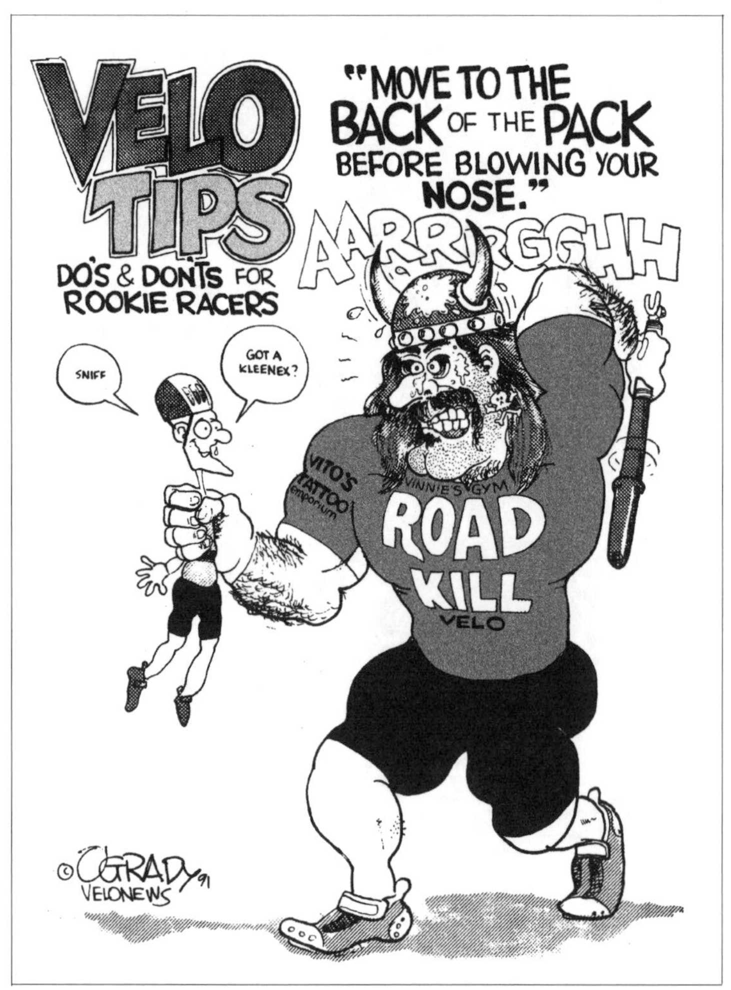
VELO TIPS
DO'S & DON'TS FOR ROOKIE RACERS
"MOVE TO THE BACK OF THE PACK BEFORE BLOWING YOUR NOSE."
AARRRGGHH
SNIFF
GOT A KLEENEX?
VITO'S TATTOO emporium
VINNIE'S GYM
ROAD KILL
VELO
©O'GRADY '91 VELONEWS

4-8-91 You may think it's funny, but it's snot.

WITH OUR DISCOUNT AND YOUR FREQUENT-FLIER MILES, YOUR TICKET WILL BE A MERE $1 98...
... PLUS A PIDDLING $799 98 TO CARRY YOUR BIKE.
SKYHI
AIRLINES
Patrick O'Grady cartoon
©O'GRADY '91 VELONEWS

4-22-91 If that were a golf bag, it would fly for free. But if he were into golf, he'd probably be the pilot.

... IT'S THE RIGHT BEER NOWW...
KAPOWKAPOWPOW!
NOT IN SMITH COUNTY TEXAS IT AIN'T, BUBBA.
...PAGING DR. WELBY ...
©O'GRADY '91 VELONEWS

5-6-91 Coors Light was nearly run out of alcohol-free Smith County, Texas, during the Beauty and the Beast racing weekend. The revenuers finally let them race...in generic jerseys, with tape covering the Coors logos on their bikes. I am not making this up.

COME AND...
CHOMP!
... get it?
HELMET SPONSORS
PRO
©O'GRADY '91 VELONEWS
Patrick O'Grady cartoon

5-20-91 Pros protested mandatory helmets, which they felt were hot and rendered them unrecognizable to the public and therefore less marketable to sponsors, who give them money for wearing stuff. Like helmets.

HEY BOB... I SEEM TO HAVE PICKED UP AN IMPERFECTION IN MY LENS...
HI MOM
©O'GRADY '91 VELONEWS
ESPN
TEAM TWIT
DU PONT
Patrick O'Grady cartoon

6-3-91 The much-maligned brain-buckets came in handy during the Tour DuPont, however.

OK, DUDE, I'LL TRADE YOU ALEXI AND THE BOSTISAURUS FOR YOUR LANCE ARMSTRONG!
NO WAY, DUDE...
OOPS, THERE GOES GREG, OFF THE BACK AGAIN...
©O'GRADY'91 VELONEWS
Patrick O'Grady cartoon

6-24-91 Shaklee and other teams were doing trading cards. I was doing gratuitous LeMond jokes.

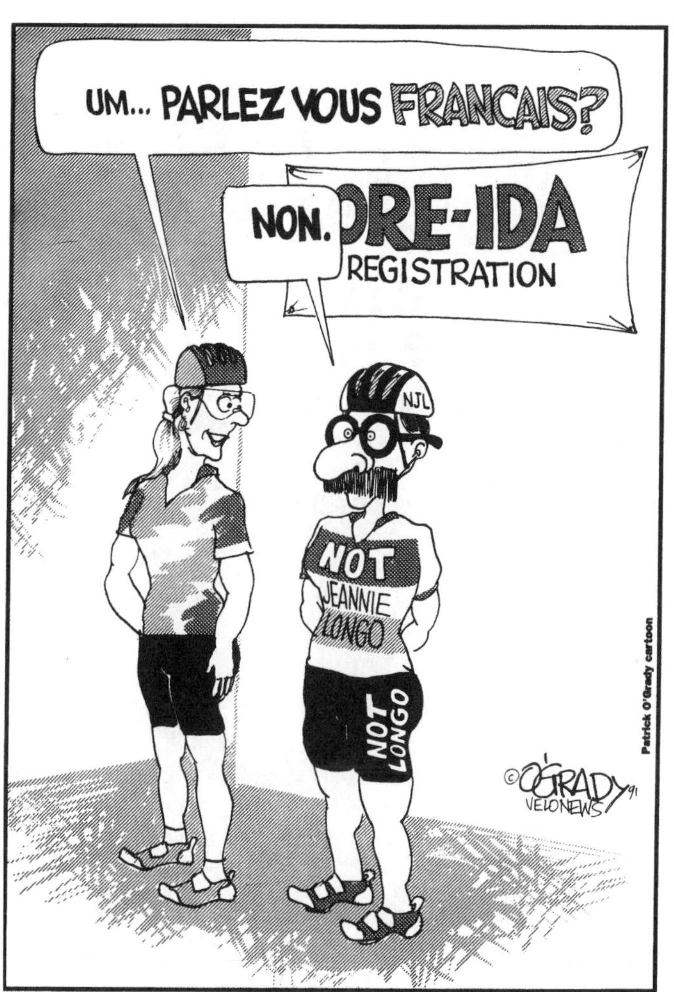
UM... PARLEZ VOUS FRANCAIS?
NON.
ORE-IDA REGISTRATION
NJL
NOT JEANNIE LONGO
NOT LONGO
©O'GRADY'91 VELONEWS
Patrick O'Grady cartoon

7-8-91 The formerly retired Jeannie Longo entered the Ore-Ida—and won it—as "Jane Ciprelli."

cy·clo·cross (sī'klō krôs) n. [< Gr. psycho, a loony + cross, an affliction one has to bear.]
1. used to repel demons that encourage cyclists to race skinny-tired bikes in obstacle-strewn mud puddles in the dead of winter.
BACK! O UNCLEAN SPIRIT!
AW C'MON DUDE... IT'S FUN...
Mephisto's MUD SHARKS
Patrick O'Grady cartoon
©O'GRADY '91 VELONEWS

8-21-91 I discovered cyclo-cross in New Mexico, and in no time could easily make the podium in a three-rider field.

WHAT REALLY GOES ON IN A RAAM RIDER'S HEAD
OBOY! ANOTHER SADDLE SORE!
WHACK WHACK
HAAHAHAH! I LOVE IT!
I THINK I'LL GO FOR A RIDE AFTERWARD AAHAHAHAHEEHEE HARHARCHORTLE GIBBER
MORE MILES! THIS RACE IS TOO @#!!*! SHORT!
LACTIC ACID
SLEEP IS FOR PANSIES! AAAHAAHAAHH
Patrick O'Grady cartoon
©O'GRADY '91 VELONEWS

8-26-91 This isn't true. There is absolutely nothing going on in a RAAM rider's head.

SURE, IT'S A TECHNICAL COURSE, BUT HEY! IF IT WEREN'T CHALLENGING, IT WOULDN'T BE ANY FUN!
NOW IF YOU'LL JUST SIGN THIS WAIVER...
PAY THE BEARER ONE SOUL
BEELZEBUB'S BLAST FURNACE OFF-ROAD RACE
START
© O'GRADY '91 VELONEWS

9-9-91 This is where Bailey's Bailout at Vail really ends up.

IT'S VITAL TO DRESS PROPERLY FOR WINTER RIDING... NOTE THE NEOPRENE MASK, THE LAYERS OF POLYPRO AND WOOL, THE THICK WINDPROOF PANTS, THE BOOTIES...
SO START RIDING.
CAN'T GET A LEG OVER THE TOP TUBE...
© O'GRADY '91 VELONEWS
Patrick O'Grady cartoon

10-18-91 The good news is, when you crash on the ice, it doesn't hurt.

cross-training (krôs-trān-iŋ) n. any form of exertion that fails to include two wheels and shoes you can't walk in. (see winter)
DEAR? HOW'D YOU LIKE TO GO FOR A SHORT RUN?
OUCH
OUCH
OUCH
VELO JUNKIES
VELOMART SPRING '92 STUFF YOU CAN'T USE NOW
VELO JUNKIES
Patrick O'Grady cartoon
©O'GRADY '91 VELONEWS

12-16-91 This one was popular in the Bible Belt, where several readers wanted to belt me with their Bibles.

THE USCF WANTS YOU TO BE A BIKE RACER

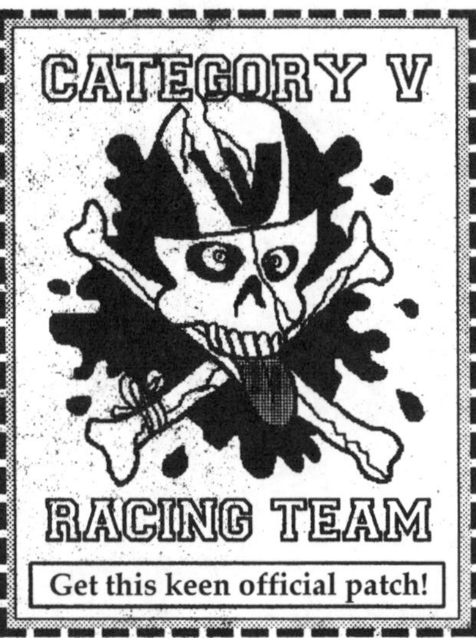
CATEGORY V
RACING TEAM
Get this keen official patch!

Tired of hearing the same old taunts on club rides? "Hey, Fred, whyncha try riding a straight line for once? Hey, Fred, quit half-wheeling me! HEY, FRED, LOOK OUT, AAAIIIEEEEE!" Well, don't waste another minute picking gravel out of your scalp — join the USCF's Cat. V Racing Team today! Imagine the look on what's left of that wiseguy's face when you say, "Hey, dude, I'm a racer too!"

SPONSORED BY

Free Spirit Bikes
Kevlar jerseys
Neosporin
Bactine
The Plasma Center and the AMA*

* Just kidding. Please don't hurt me. I have no health insurance. Thank you.

©O'GRADY '92 VELONEWS

1-20-92 A reader wrote to ask where he could buy this patch. Sorry, son...you have to earn this one.

©O'GRADY'92 VELONEWS
DUUUDE! YOU GOT THE HOCK SHOX™!
WHEN YA GONNA INSTALL 'EM? HUH? HUH DUDE?
NO TIME SOON, DUDE... I HADDA PAWN MY BIKE TA BUY 'EM...
WANNA GO BOWLING OR SOMETHIN?
DIRT DAWG
Patrick O'Grady cartoon

2-10-92 Rock Shox's promotions people went the patch guy one better by actually making "Hock Shox" badges.

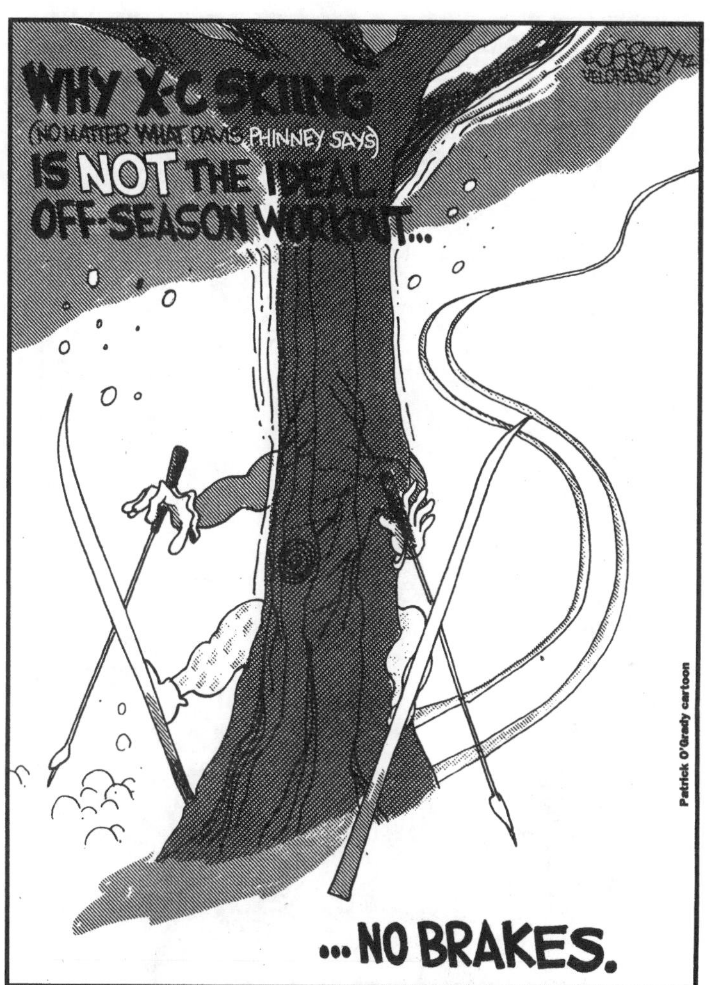
©O'GRADY'92 VELONEWS
WHY X-C SKIING
(NO MATTER WHAT DAVIS PHINNEY SAYS)
IS NOT THE IDEAL OFF-SEASON WORKOUT...
...NO BRAKES.
Patrick O'Grady cartoon

3-2-92 Like any good dog, I ski from tree to tree.

THE FIRST PACELINE OF THE NEW SEASON...
OOPS
AAAIIEE! @#!!*@!!
SHREK! @#!!*@!!
YOWL! @#!!*@!!
CRUNCH
CLATTER
SNAP
HOOK
SMASH
CLANG
THUD
... AND THE SECOND ONE.
©O'GRADY '92 VELONEWS
OOPS
WHERE'S THE @#!!! BIG RING?
YOU GONNA TAKE A PULL OR WHAT?
HMPH
Patrick O'Grady cartoon

3-23-92 Inspired by a mishap during an early-season training ride.

JEEZ, IT'S TRUE! ROLL'S RACING OFF-ROAD! THERE HE IS!
AND THERE!
AND THERE!
AND THERE...
©O'GRADY '92 VELONEWS
Patrick O'Grady cartoon

4-6-92 Bob Roll put a lot of himself into the '92 Cactus Cup. About a quart's worth.

WILL RACE FOR FOOD
FORGET IT, DEAR... I'VE SEEN THESE GUYS EAT.

5-4-92 Cyclists lose races, sponsors and their tempers. But they never lose their appetites.

MEANWHILE, BACK AT DOC FRANKENSTEIN'S...
YO, OCH? FRANK. YEP – IGOR BLEW IT ON THE BRAIN AGAIN. YEAH, IT'S @#!!*@! HAPPENED BEFORE... WHAT, YOU NEVER WATCH THE LATE SHOW? JEEZ... GET A LIFE.
WHAT?
YEAH, IT'S UNDER WARRANTY...
I VISH NOW TO PLAY HOCKEY.
MOTOROLA
MOTOROLA
DIEHARD
©O'GRADY '92 VELONEWS
Patrick O'Grady cartoon

6-1-92 Michel Zanoli took a swing at a TV-motorbike driver, then connected with Davis Phinney in stage nine of the Du Pont. Hasta la vista, baby.

YAAAARRRRRG GGGGHHHHHH!!!
RATATATATATAT ATATATATATAT
DIE! DIE! DIE!
WHUT, MOMMA? OH, IT'S JUST BILLY BOB... HE'S A MITE PUT OUT 'CUZ TH' TEEVEE'S SHOWIN' A BUNCHA FAIRIES ON BIKES 'STEADA TH' TRACTOR PULL...
ESPN
LOOKS LOIKE ANOTHERR FOINE FIELD BRIAN...
Patrick O'Grady cartoon
©O'GRADY 92 VELONEWS

6-22-92 I feel the same way about golf.

OK, WHO'S NEXT HERE... SIR JEFF OF EVANSHINE! EVANSHINE? WHAT? HE'S AT HIS LAWYER'S? JEEZ... NO WONDER THEY CALL IT OLYMPIC "TRIALS"...
PULL
PEE
USCF
©O'GRADY 92 VELONEWS

7-6-92 Junior world road champ Jeff Evanshine missed a random drug test and drew a three-month suspension from USCF on the evening of the '92 nationals. He appealed the decision, noting, "The USCF sucks, and you can print that." We did.

ARRIBA, ARRIBA Y LEJOS!
WELL, I'D SAY THAT EXPLAINS A FEW THINGS...
Phone
Phone
LE WHO?
VELONEWS
INDURAIN KICKS BUTT PROLOGUE
Banesto
©O'GRADY'92 VELONEWS

7-20-92 Here comes Big Mig...

©O'GRADY'92 VELONEWS
LEMOND
Patrick O'Grady cartoon

8-10-92 ...and there goes Big Greg.

©O'GRADY'92 VELONEWS
HEY MISTER! WHERE'D ALL THE BIG KIDS GO?
TRY OVER THERE BY THE MEDAL STAND, KID... IF YOU HURRY YOU CAN CATCH THE CLOSING CEREMONIES.
PUFF
PUFF
PUFF
SQUEAK
RATTLE
USA
Patrick O'Grady cartoon

8-24-92 The 1992 Olympics wasn't exactly a gold mine for U.S. cycling.

... MEANWHILE, AT NORBA NATIONALS IN 2032...
©O'GRADY'92 VELONEWS
... AND IT LOOKS LIKE... YES, IT'S NED OVEREND! HE JUST GETS BETTER, NOT OLDER, RIGHT CHARLIE? CHARLIE? SOMEBODY TURN UP LITSKY'S HEARING AID FOR CHRISSAKES...
HEE HEE HEE... WONDER IF THEY LET OL' JOHNNY T. WATCH TV IN THAT NURSING HOME...
SPECIALIZED
FINISH
Patrick O'Grady cartoon

9-21-92 Fortunately, Ned Overend was providing plenty of inspiration for those of us in need of it.

MUD STUDS
BIFF
CYCLO-CROSS BARRIERS INC.
©O'GRADY'92
MAD DOG MEDIA
Patrick O'Grady cartoon

Q: What's the last thing to go through a cyclo-crosser's mind after he careens down a muddy hill into a staked-down barrier at 30 mph?
A: His butt.

11-9-92 Okay, so it's an old joke. So am I, and that's me up there.

©O'GRADY'92 VELONEWS
SO ANYWAY, I HAD THIS LIKE TOTALLY HEINOUS DREAM ... I WAS RACING, OK, BUT IN THIS LIKE TOTALLY BLANK JERSEY!
HADDA PAY ENTRY FEES, BUY ALL MY OWN STUFF... I WOKE UP INNA COLD SWEAT.
THAT REMINDS ME, DUDE... YOUR SPONSOR CALLED—SOMETHING ABOUT CHAPTER 11...
YOU WRITIN' A BOOK OR SOMETHING?
ephemeral
TRANSITORY VELO
Patrick O'Grady cartoon

12-14-92 It wouldn't be so bad when sponsors go away if they didn't always insist on taking their money with them.

©O'GRADY'93 VELONEWS
HELL, I THOUGHT THIS CYCLO-CROSS STUFF WAS SUPPOSED TO BE HARD! YEEEEEHAWWWW...
OH, IT IS, IT IS... AND GETTING HARDER ALL THE TIME...
FAT TIRE flyers
TRIPLE RING VELO
Patrick O'Grady cartoon

1-18-93 Mark Howe rode where the rest of us ran during the '92 'cross nationals in Golden.

IT'S NOT "ALL-RIGHTA", OK? NOT!
RELAX... HERE, HAVE A POTATO...
ORE-IDA
SICK OF 30 MINUTE CRITS VELO
TEAM
GRETA'S BIG & TALL SHOP
RIP ORE-IDA 1993
©O'GRADY'93 MAD DOG MEDIA
Patrick O'Grady cartoon

3-1-93 Ore-Ida couldn't find enough co-sponsors to help underwrite the Idaho Women's Challenge, and the race was canceled.

GET OFF THE ROAD!
BEEEEEEPPP
RIGHT HERE MAN...
GET OFF THE TRAIL!
GET OFF MY CASE...
GET OFF YOUR ASS!
AWN DUUUDE... THIS IS MY REST DAY.
ANY MORE CHIPS?
DAILY DAILY
BIKE BAN PROPOSED
©O'GRADY'93 MAD DOG MEDIA
Patrick O'Grady cartoon

3-22-93 We tend to ignore anyone who isn't actively trying to kill us, right now.

©O'GRADY'93 MAD DOG MEDIA
FFFIIISSSSS...
OOF!
HEY!
WIDGET
DOOHICKEY CORP
WHAP
...SO WHEN THE QUESTION OF SPONSOR RECOGNITION CAME UP, WE THOUGHT, HEY! WHY LIMIT "PUMP" TECHNOLOGY TO SHOES AND HELMETS?
I LIKE IT, I LIKE IT...
TOUR de BUCK$
CHECK IT OUT MAN... GREG IN THE OFF-SEASON... AAAHAAHAAHAHAH
OLD GUYS WHO GET FAT
Patrick O'Grady cartoon

4-5-93 Reebok's Pump technology was turning up everywhere.

BREAKER BREAKER...
GOOD BUDDY, YOU GOTCHER EARS ON?
GO, BREAKER... WHAT'S YOUR HANDLE?
THEY CALL ME "THE SPONSOR," GOOD BUDDY, AND I'M GONE! SEVENS 'N' THREES TO YA... CATCH YA ONNA FLIPFLOP BABBLEYAMMER
WHERE'S ZANOLI WHEN YOU NEED HIM?
MOTOROLA
MOTOROLA
MOTOROLA
Patrick O'Grady cartoon
©O'GRADY 93 MAD DOG MEDIA

4-26-93 Motorola pulls the plug.

Patrick O'Grady cartoon
SIR? IT'S LITSKY AGAIN... HE SAYS MAJOR TAYLOR NEEDS A VELODROME, BOB COOK REQUIRES A MOUNTAIN, AND THE DOWNHILL YOU PUT TOGETHER FOR LUCIFER MAY HAVE BEEN "AWESOME" A MILLION YEARS AGO, BUT NOW IT'S "BOGUS." ... ANY REPLY?
HIMSELF
FINE. ANYTHING. JUST AS LONG AS HE STOPS CALLING ME "DUDE."
©O'GRADY 93 MAD DOG MEDIA
SO LONG, CHARLIE...

6-14-93 Charlie Litsky dies of a massive heart attack at age 33. Things got a lot quieter on the NORBA circuit.

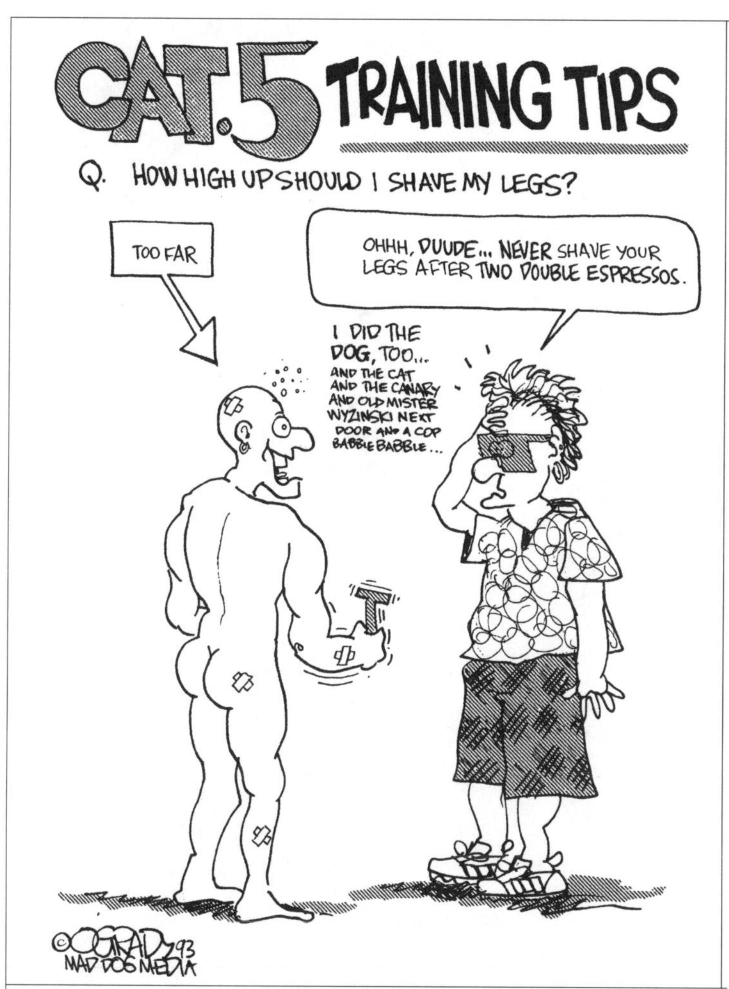
CAT. 5 TRAINING TIPS
Q. HOW HIGH UP SHOULD I SHAVE MY LEGS?
TOO FAR
OHHH, DUUDE... NEVER SHAVE YOUR LEGS AFTER TWO DOUBLE ESPRESSOS.
I DID THE DOG, TOO... AND THE CAT AND THE CANARY AND OLD MISTER WYZINSKI NEXT DOOR AND A COP BABBLE BABBLE...
©O'GRADY '93 MAD DOG MEDIA

6-28-93 I can't be the only guy who's ever pondered this question.

YYAAARRRGGHHHH!!!
LOOKS LIKE JOHN HEARD THERE'S NO SAME-DAY TOUR COVERAGE THIS YEAR...
CATCH IT, DUDE! ESPN AN' PSN GOTS MUCHO MOUNTAIN BIKEAGE!
...AN' I GOT CABLE!
ROAD TOADZ
©O'GRADY '93 MAD DOG MEDIA

7-12-93 TV was headed off road, where it was easier for bonehead cameramen to find giant sunflowers to draw the viewer's eye away from whatever those guys on the bikes are doing back there.

©O'GRADY'93
MAD DOG MEDIA
FIRST, THAT LEMOND PERSON, NOW THIS... IT IS NOTHING SHORT OF MORTIFYING!
... WHY, I HAVE DERAILLEURS OLDER THAN HIM!
... WHERE IS MY DOMESTIQUE? I REQUIRE A BAND-AID...
LE TOUR C'EST MOI
euro dogs
HOWDY FROM PLANO, TEXAS
LE TOUR
LE TOUR
CLICK
CLACK
CLICK
CLACK

7-26-93 Lance Armstrong was making a point across the pond.

YOU SHOULDA SEEN JULI COME THROUGH, DUDE... SHE WAS FLYING.
SO WHAT, DUDE... SHE'S ALWAYS FLYING...
YEAH, WELL, THIS TIME SHE HAD A BIG RED "S" ON HER JERSEY...
... SAID SOMETHIN' ABOUT BEIN' REAL BUSY SINCE SUPERMAN SNUFFED IT... WONDER IF RUTHIE CAN GET HER HANDS ON ANY KRYPTONITE?
©O'GRADY'93
MAD DOG MEDIA

8-9-93 Back home, meanwhile, Juli Furtado was faster than a speeding bullet.

MEANWHILE, AT MASTERS NATIONALS, THE GUY WHO HADN'T HEARD ABOUT THE VENUE CHANGE PLUGGED ALONG IN THE TIME TRIAL...
©O'GRADY '93 MAD DOG MEDIA
JEEZ, I'D HEARD ABOUT THE HUMIDITY IN ST. LOUIS, BUT THIS IS RIDICULOUS...
YEAH, BUT THEN YOU DON'T HAVE TO LUG AROUND THAT HEAVY WATER BOTTLE...
SPEEDO
Patrick O'Grady cartoon

8-30-93 Flooding forced a course change for the masters-nationals time trial. I figure at least one guy didn't get the word.

DUDES! BE THE FIRST IN YOUR PELOTON TO GET THE OFFICIAL LANCE ARMSTRONG™ STEM STATUE!*
BLESS ME, LANCE, FOR I HAVE SINNED...
HANDCRAFTED IN PLANO TEXAS, OF TITANIUM & TESTOSTERONE, THIS HANDSOME IDOL (SUITABLE FOR WORSHIP) GIVES YOU THE SAME VIEW OF LANCE THAT THE PROS GET... JUST ZIP-TIE LANCE TO YOUR STEM AND WATCH HIM BURN UP THE ROAD!
...I NEVER TRAIN, BUT I STILL WANNA WIN...
MOTOROLA
JUST SEND $29.95 TO OUR LADY OF THE GENERAL CLASSIFICATION, 1993 LACTIC ACID WAY, VOTWOMAX, TX. 11111 - QUANTITIES LIMITED.
©O'GRADY '93 MAD DOG MEDIA
Patrick O'Grady cartoon

9-20-93 Lance wins the world's, and American cycling gets a desperately needed new icon.

MEANWHILE, AT INTERBIKE IN VEGAS...
©O'GRADY '93 MAD DOG MEDIA
'SCUSE ME, I'M WITH VELONEWS... WHAT'S WITH THE LINE? YOU GUYS WAITING ON LEMOND? ARMSTRONG? EDDY MERCKX?
FORGET THEM, MAN... WE'RE AFTER COFFEE.
♪ BACK AGAIN, SIR?
SHUT UP AND POUR.
YOU OUGHTA SEE MURPHY'S S-WORKS ESPRESSO MUG ... IT SEATS FOUR.
SAY, WANNA LOOKIT OUR LINE? FULL-SUSPENSION TITANIUM HYBRID INLINE APRES-BIKE WEAR... WITH GRIP SHIFT.
I COULDN'T QUIT AFTER THE SHIRT WENT... NOOOO, I HAD TO DRAW JUST ONCE MORE TO AN INSIDE STRAIGHT...
AND THEN THERE WAS SPEC'ING SUNTOUR...
VELONEWS
WILL REP FOR CHIPS
Patrick O'Grady cartoon

10-4-93 The most popular product at the Interbike show? Coffee.

©O'GRADY '93 MAD DOG MEDIA
CONGRATULATIONS, DUDE... LET'S SEE THOSE @#!!!*?@! MOUNTAIN BIKERS BUNNY-HOP THIS COURSE!
PSYCHO CROSS
BARRIERS... NEED... MORE... BARRIERS! NNGGHHH
MUD!
ANNGH
MORE HILLS ALL UPHILL

12-13-93 With mountain bikers pouring into 'cross races, course designers struggled to level the playing field.

NEXT, THE LATEST IN THE NANCY KERRIGAN -TONYA HARDING DRAMA...
THAT'S IT! THAT'S HOW WE GET SOME MEDIA! ANDY PAYS CLAUDIO TO WHACK MIGUEL JUST BEFORE THE TOUR! 60 MINUTES! 20/20! MAYBE... MAYBE... OPRAH!
SORRY... STILL WON'T COVER IT ... TRY CALLING FOX.
SNAP!
THIS SPACE FOR RENT
WHO U. CYCLING
VELO ? ANONYMOUS
GS OBSCURITY
WHATSIDAT
© O'GRADY '94 MAD DOG MEDIA

2-7-94 Time to kneecap a few TV execs, maybe?

I'M REALLY PISSED OFF ABOUT THIS CHANGING ALL THE CATEGORIES...
... BUST MY BUTT TO MAKE CAT. 3 AND ALL OF A SUDDEN THEY CALL IT SOMETHING ELSE...
AW, C'MON, DUDE... BE A "SPORT!"
AAAAHAAHAAHA HAHAHAHAHAAA...

NOT VERY SPORTSMANLIKE OF YOU, DUDE...
MOAN
© O'GRADY '94 MAD DOG MEDIA

3-7-94 One lame joke deserves another.

© O'GRADY '94
MAD DOG MEDIA
THANKS TO HAL
GOD, I LOVE MARCH.
TEAM BRONCHITIS
DOG TROTTERS
HOME

3-21-94 Springtime in the Rockies.

DUUUDE! WHAT A RAGIN' RACE, HUH? WAAAY COOL COURSES, THE TOMES SLEW ALL, AN' JULI... WOW, DUDE, LIKE SHE MUST BE FROM KRYPTON OR SOMETHIN'! IS THE CACTUS CUP THE COOLEST RACE OR WHAT?
TEAM Biff
Dingle
HELL YES.
GREAT RACE.
BITCHEN DUDE.
NOW SHUT THE @#!!! UP, GET THE TWEEZERS AND FILL UP THE BATHTUB WITH BACTINE.
OR I'LL KILL YOU.
FREE CLINIC
© O'GRADY '94
MAD DOG MEDIA

4-4-94 Cactus Cup can punch a few holes in your early-season program.

NORBA ANNOUNCED TODAY THAT ALL LICENSEES MUST HAVE GOATEES, REALLY STUPID HAIRCUTS AND AT LEAST ONE EARRING...
IN RELATED NEWS, RECENTLY DECLASSIFIED PENTAGON DOCUMENTS CONFIRM THAT JULI FURTADO IS ACTUALLY A NASA ANDROID INTENDED FOR EXPLORATORY MISSIONS TO THE PLANET JUPITER...
GOATEES? EVEN THE WIMMEN? DUUUUDE....
dirt DOGZ
TEAM FACEPLANT
STYLIN' DUDE MAGAZINE
©O'GRADY '94
MAD DOG MEDIA

4-25-94 Not really…it just seemed that way sometimes.

WITH THE FAMED "OBREE POSITION" IN JEOPARDY, WORK CONTINUES NIGHT AND DAY TOWARD DEVELOPING A SUITABLE REPLACEMENT...
BUT I'M TELLIN' YER, GRAEME, IT'LL WORK! AND IT'S AERO' AS HELL— Y'BREAK THE WIND WI'YER BUM!
I ALREADY BREAK WIND WI'ME BUM, Y'TWIT! @#!!*!
TRY AGAIN...
PROTOTYPE # 6129301
AIR FLOW
REFLECTIVE NAVIGATIONAL AID (MIRROR)
BUM
REAR
FRONT
FINISH LINE, RECORDS & FAME
©O'GRADY '94
MAD DOG MEDIA

5-16-94 Did you ever get the idea that Graeme cared less about setting records than about annoying the UCI?

©O'GRADY '94
MAD DOG MEDIA
STOP
JOHN STENNER
1965–1994
OLD GUYS WHO GET FAT IN WINTER RACING TEAM

6-13-94 Time trialist John Stenner is killed in a car-bike mishap.

WORKING OVERTIME AT THE BANESTO GARAGE...
©O'GRADY '94
MAD DOG MEDIA
PEEEEEEYEW!
THIS SUMBITCH IS BURNED OUT!
OPEN A @#!!*@! WINDOW, BOY...
YEAH... SUCKER WAS ACTUALLY GOIN' BACKWARD THERE FOR A WHILE... GOTTA BE A SHORT SOMEWHERES...
IT'S STILL TALKIN' BOSS...
WHERE'S THEM JUMPER CABLES AT, BUBBA?
DEFEAT... IT'S NEW TO ME. BEEP, CLICK, WHIRRRRR... DEFEAT... IT'S NEWW TOOO MEEEE
Banesto
CAUTION
DELCO

6-27-94 Big Mig blew a gasket in the Giro. Even Ferraris wind up in the shop now and then.

ON A WHIM, JEANNE GOLAY DECIDES TO WEAR ALL THE JERSEYS SHE WON AT NATIONALS...
GETTING THEM OFF AGAIN WILL REQUIRE SOMETHING A LITTLE MORE SUBSTANTIAL...
SOMEBODY CALL 911 ... AND MAKE SURE THEY'VE GOT THE JAWS OF LIFE.
I GOTTA GO TO THE BATHROOM...
SATURN
© O'GRADY 94 MAD DOG MEDIA

7-11-94 Jeanne Golay had collected eight of these jerseys by July 1994.

THEY SAY MASSAGE CAN HELP SPEED RECOVERY...
WHOEVER "THEY" ARE...
EVER CONSIDER, SAY, STRETCHING NOW AND THEN?
De Sade
© O'GRADY 94 MAD DOG MEDIA

7-25-94 Talk about getting rubbed the wrong way....

WITH THE '94 TOUR IN THE BAG, WORK BEGINS ON NEXT YEAR'S ROUTE...

©O'GRADY '94
MAD DOG MEDIA

OK, SO WE ARE AGREED... PROLOGUE UP MONT VENTOUX; ANOTHER CHANNEL CROSSING, BUT OUTSIDE THE "CHUNNEL"; NO @#!!*@!?!! TIME TRIALS; A CYCLO-CROSS ON L'ALPE D'HUEZ; AND EVERYTHING ELSE IN THE ALPS. ANYTHING ELSE?

A MAILLOT JAUNE WOVEN OF LEAD, JUST IN CASE...
...AND MORE GREASE IN THE CORNERS THIS TIME.
COURSE PROFILE
STAGE ONE

8-8-94 Indurain wins his fourth Tour by a huge margin, and some sort of handicap is considered.

MEANWHILE, TIME AND SPACE COLLIDE AT JUNIOR NATIONALS...
©O'GRADY '94
MAD DOG MEDIA
HERE'S YOUR MEDAL, SON... CONGRATULATIONS ON A JOB WELL DONE!
COOL! I COULDA SWORN I WUZ LAST...
ARE YOU SURE THIS IS RIGHT?
SHUTTUP- I'M TIMING! ONE THOUSAND ONE, ONE THOUSAND SIX, ONE THOUSAND... AW, SHOOT...
URP
TIMER
DO NOT DISTURB
FOOD MART
TEAM TWO-TON
GOBBLER
CHIX ON A STICK
höggen dawgs
DEEP FAT ICE CREAM
BUBBA'S PORK RINDS
Cheez

8-7-94 There were some questions about the accuracy of the timing at junior nationals.

CYCLO-CROSS BUILDS HANDLING SKILLS AND FITNESS ... OR, SOMETIMES, IT SIMPLY PUTS YOU IN A MUD BOG WITH RUTHLESS LUNATICS WHO ALREADY POSSESS THESE THINGS...
©O'GRADY '94 MAD DOG MEDIA
HEY, DUDE... YOU'RE SUPPOSED TO DISMOUNT FOR THEM BARRIERS...
WELL, I'M CERTAINLY OFF THE BIKE NOW...
BOG TROTTERS
MUD MASTERS

11-7-94 Mud: It's not just for breakfast anymore.

INSANITY CLAUS(E)...
©O'GRADY '94 MAD DOG MEDIA
MERRY XMAS, VELOSNOOZERS
GET OUTA THE WAY, DUDES... UNLESS YOU WANNA STOCKING FULLA BUSTED COLLARBONES FOR CHRIS'MUS!
GOD I'M GLAD I ATE THEM @#!!! REINDEER...
HO HO HO EXPRESS
ELVES RULE
NORTH POLE VELO
RUDOLPH

12-12-94 This saved me a ton of money on Christmas cards.

©O'GRADY'95 MAD DOG MEDIA
THE END THE LEMOND STORY
OLD GUYS WHO GET FAT IN WINTER RACING TEAM
BUBBA'S BBQ
VELONEWS
LEMOND QUITS
90 TOUR
87 TOUR
GREG LEMOND'S COMPLETE BOOK OF BICYCLING

I-16-95 The LeMond era ends.

HEY, IS IT RAINING OR SOMETHING?
WELL, KINDA... SEEMS LIKE IT'S ALWAYS "RAINING" WHENEVER WE RIDE UNDER ZAPATA ESPINOZA'S WINDOW...
JEEZ, THAT GUY MUST DRINK A LOT OF COFFEE...
RANGE ROVER
STUPIDIUM
ROAD TOADS
COLNAGO
©O'GRADY'95 MAD DOG MEDIA

2-6-95 *Mountain Bike* editor Zapata Espinoza was busily making friends among the roadie community.

©O'GRADY '95
MAD DOG MEDIA
♫
euro CROSS
MK MUDDER FUGGIN KIKKENASSOVICH
JEEZ, I HATE THAT GUY...
USA

2-27-95 America continued its winning ways at cyclo-cross world's.

OH, MAANNN... I'M NOT READY FOR HILLS YET!
I GOTTA WORK UP TO THIS... MORE BASE MILES, BEEF UP THE WEIGHTS, MAYBE THROW IN A FEW INTERVALS...
FRED... IT'S A SPEED BUMP.
GOD, I'M GOING ANAEROBIC ALREADY!
BEEP BEEP BEEP BEEP
©O'GRADY '95 MAD DOG MEDIA

3-27-95 This was my birthday, and I was obviously feeling my age.

LENNIE, I THINK YOU'RE STARTING TO OVERDO THE WEIGHTS A BIT...
GEE, DO YA THINK SO, GEORGE?
© O'GRADY '95 MAD DOG MEDIA
YEAH, LENNIE... I THINK SO.
DOES THIS MEAN I CAN'T HAVE NO RABBITS, GEORGE?
I JUST WANNA HOLD 'UM AND PET 'UM AND LOVE 'UM AND SQUEEZE 'UM...
PEC'S GYM

4-10-95 Lots of cartoonists have done *Of Mice and Men* riffs, and I am nothing if not imitative.

THERE'S A NEW SHERIFF IN TOWN, PODNAH!
YEAH, BUT IT'S STARTIN' TO LOOK A LOT LIKE THAT SAME OL' RODEO... URRRGHH...
MARSHAL COORS LIGHT GOOD RIDDANCE RIP 1994
CHEVY L.A.
CROAK
OUCH
© O'GRADY '95 MAD DOG MEDIA

4-24-95 The new fastest gun in town was the Chevy-L.A. Sheriff's team.

MEANWHILE, AT THE TOUR DU PONT...
IMAGINE MY SURPRISE ... ALL THESE YEARS I AM THINKING HE IS JUST A CARTOON!
POW
WHERE'S THAT TOUR DE FRANCE THING AT?
euro dogs
APOLOGIES TO MARVEL & CAPTAIN AMERICA
© O'GRADY '95 MAD DOG MEDIA

5-22-95 Lance was kicking much Euro' butt, and I was having yet another flashback to childhood literature.

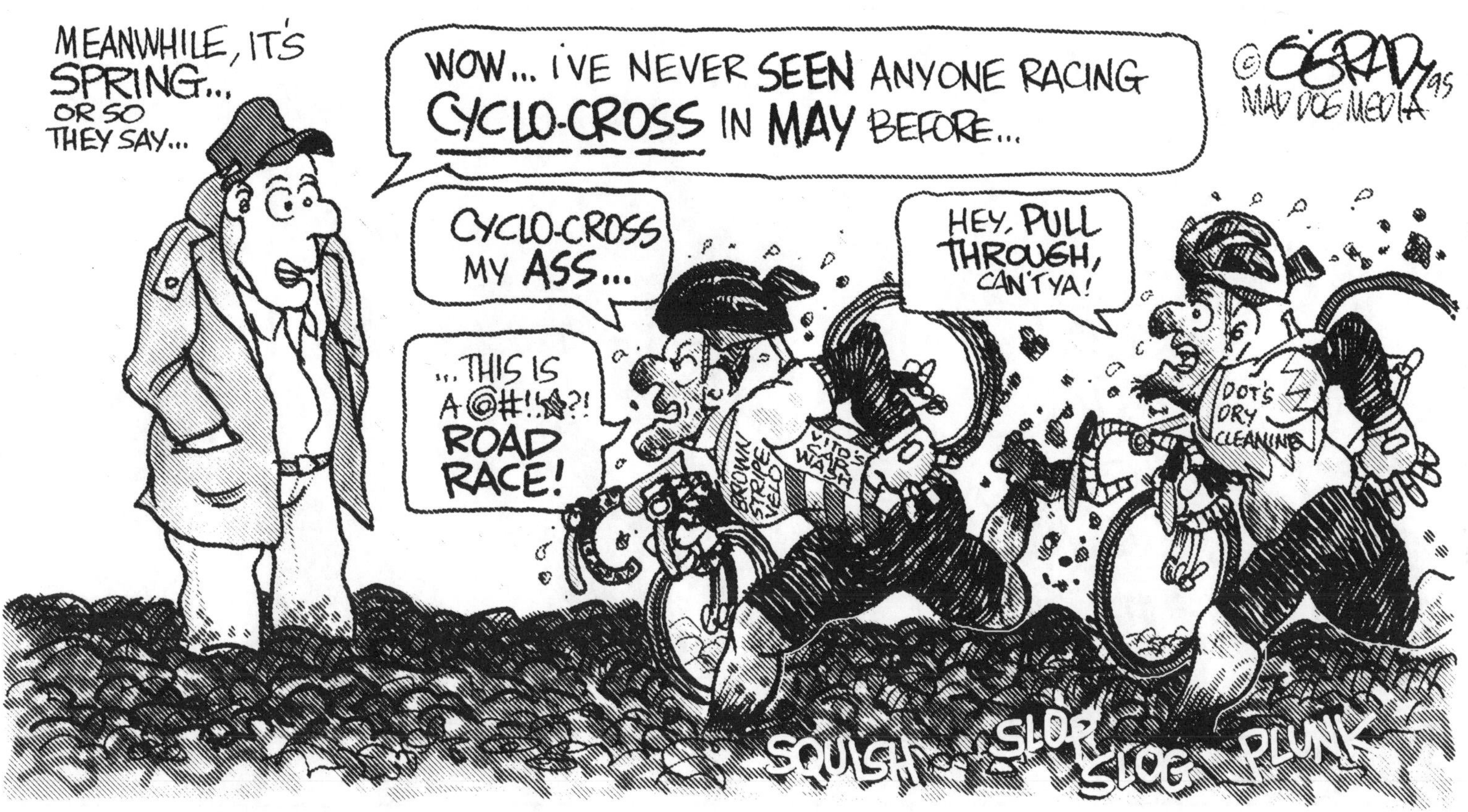
MEANWHILE, IT'S SPRING... OR SO THEY SAY...
WOW... I'VE NEVER SEEN ANYONE RACING CYCLO-CROSS IN MAY BEFORE...
© O'GRADY '95 MAD DOG MEDIA
CYCLO-CROSS MY ASS...
...THIS IS A @#!!$?! ROAD RACE!
HEY, PULL THROUGH, CAN'TYA!
BROWN STRIPE VELO
VITO'S CAR WASH
DOT'S DRY CLEANING
SQUISH
SLOP
SLOG
PLUNK

6-5-95 It was another one of those springs. Nuclear submarines reported better weather at the bottom of the North Atlantic.

ARE YOU NUTS OR SOMETHING? CAN'T YOU SEE WE'RE DOING A @#!!☆@!!!?!! MOUNTAIN BIKE RACE HERE?
HE'S GOT THE ONLY GOOD LINE, TOO, DUDE...
©O'GRADY 95 MAD DOG MEDIA
I'M NOT SURE, BUT I THINK I'VE BIFFED IT...

6-19-95 There are drawbacks to holding mountain-bike races on ski mountains. This is one of them.

DON'T TELL ME... LET ME GUESS: FIRST SUNNY DAY IN SIX WEEKS, A FOUR-HOUR RIDE, AND ... ... NO SUNSCREEN.
HA, HA... FILL THE BATHTUB WITH BUTTER, PLEASE...
© O'GRADY 95 MAD DOG MEDIA

7-3-95 Of course, the sun comes out eventually, and we handle it with the same good sense we employ when coming back from illness or injury.

... AND IN A STIRRING CEREMONY, THE MAILLOT JAUNE PASSES TO O.T.B. JACQUES, OF THE LITTLE-KNOWN TEAM BACKOPACK-ALSORAN ... THE ONLY RIDER IN THE '95 TOUR WHO WAS NOT HOSPITALIZED AFTER A CRASH, LOST IN A ROUNDABOUT, OR SIDELINED WITH FOOD POISONING.
CONGRATULATIONS ... ALL FRANCE IS VERY PROUD.
WHAT ARE YOUR PLANS?
I HOPE TO TAKE UP A SAFER PROFESSION... PERHAPS THE FOREIGN LEGION, OR BODYGUARD TO SALMAN RUSHDIE... MAYBE DEA CHIEF IN OKLAHOMA CITY...
... SAY, KNOW ANYONE WHO'D LIKE TO BUY A SLIGHTLY DAMAGED BIKE?
BACKOPACK ALSORAN
LE BLOOD BANQUE
© O'GRADY '95 MAD DOG MEDIA

7-4-95 It was an ugly Tour, and due to get uglier. Note the ultra-sensitive reference to the Oklahoma City bombing.

8-7-95 Twenty-four-year-old Fabio Casartelli, the '92 Olympic road-race gold medalist, dies in a high-speed crash.

WELL, YOU'D BEEN SAYING YOU THOUGHT THE SERIES NEEDED MORE CHALLENGING COURSES...
©O'GRADY '95 MAD DOG MEDIA
AIR HED
JEEEEZ, DUDE, I JUST WANTED TO GET RID OF THE GUY JUST AHEAD OF ME ON POINTS...
WHAM! BANG CRASH
UUUGGH! @#!!! ...YOU DID...

8-28-95 You don't want 'em changing channels, do you? Besides, blood makes the grass grow. Now get out there and die like a man.

SHRIEK!
...DON'T WORRY... IT'S ONLY A CARTOON, AFTER ALL... AND HE'S PROBABLY DREAMING IT ALL, ANYWAY.
BUY TREK TOOTHPASTE
STAR TREK
TREK
POST
© O'GRADY '95 MAD DOG MEDIA

9-18-95 Another magazine declined to run a similar cartoon, so I revised it for VeloNews. Unfortunately, the original was better.

12-11-95 Going postal: It took three tries to draw something that would keep *VeloNews* sending me checks, and the USPS from shredding them.

MAN... AND I THOUGHT THE SPECTATORS AT MOUNTAIN BIKE RACES WERE WEIRD-LOOKING...
OH REALLY? WELL, I CAN'T SAY I THINK MUCH OF YOUR RUNNING TECHNIQUE...
©O'GRADY 95 MAD DOG MEDIA
PSYCHO-CROSSERS
GLORK
SLORCH

1-15-96 The pig is not a USA Cycling executive. There's not enough in the trough for those guys at a 'cross race.

OFF-SEASON CROSS-TRAINING EVOLVES FROM SKIING, TO SKATING ... TO "SURFING."
...NNGH... CAN'T... UGH ...STOP...
MUST ... NNGH... FLAME... RRR... VELONEWS...
©O'GRADY 96 MADDOG MEDIA
http://www.ris.net/~velodog
WELCOME TO REC.BIKES. FAT.GUYS. WHONEED. TO GET. A. LIFE
ZONY
OLD GUYS WHO GET FAT IN WINTER RACING TEAM
ROCKY'S RIBS 'N' RAM
NETWITS software
PORCINI
ALE
Z

2-5-96 Peer pressure: The Fat Guy joins everyone else on the Usenet newsgroup rec.bicycles.racing in flaming *VeloNews*.

BOY, THE BUGS IS POWERFUL BIG THIS SPRING, HUH?
YUP... COLORFUL, TOO.
URP
...WANT ME T'SPLASH A LITTLE BEER ONNA WINDSHIELD?
IMPEACH HILLARY
DON'T LIKE MY DRIVING?
CRETINS 4 CHRIST
NRA
GET US OUT OF THE UN
© O'GRADY '96 MADDOGMEDIA
THANKS TO HAL

4-1-96 Meanwhile, velocidal motorists continued to collect those nifty Lycra-and-titanium hood ornaments.

YEAH, I DUNNO WHAT WE GOTTA DO... RUN ALONG, SON, CANTCHA SEE I'M BUSY HERE... TO GET THE DAMN' JUNIORS NUMBERS UP...
YUP... IT'S A MYSTERY ALL RIGHT.
HEY, POP...
... CAN I BORROW ONE OF YOUR BIKES?
... I GOT LITTLE LEAGUE PRACTICE.
MASTER DEBATER
MASTER DEBATER
©O'GRADY '96 MADDOGMEDIA

4-15-96 Predictions are tricky, but I feel okay about this one: The next American to win three Tours will not be a master's racer. So take a kid riding.

MY MY MY... ZAT IS A NASTY SADDLE SORE YOU'VE DEVELOPED... PERHAPS YOU'D BETTER HAVE IT "LANCED."
OHH, SHUT UP.
...AS EEF ZAT TEXAN ISN'T ENOUGH OF A PAIN IN ZE ASS.
DOKTOR
FLECHE WALLONNE
euros
©OSGRAD 96
MAD DOG MEDIA

5-13-96 This was really disgusting in color.

MEANWHILE, ON THE WORLD CUP CIRCUIT...
ACH... HOW CLUMSY OF ME...
euro
NO COOLIN
HAULINZE ass
BUMP
... SEE YOU IN ATLANTA, NO?
... NO.
MAD DOG MEDIA

5-27-96 American mountain bikers were finding the road to the Atlanta Olympic Games a wee bit rocky.

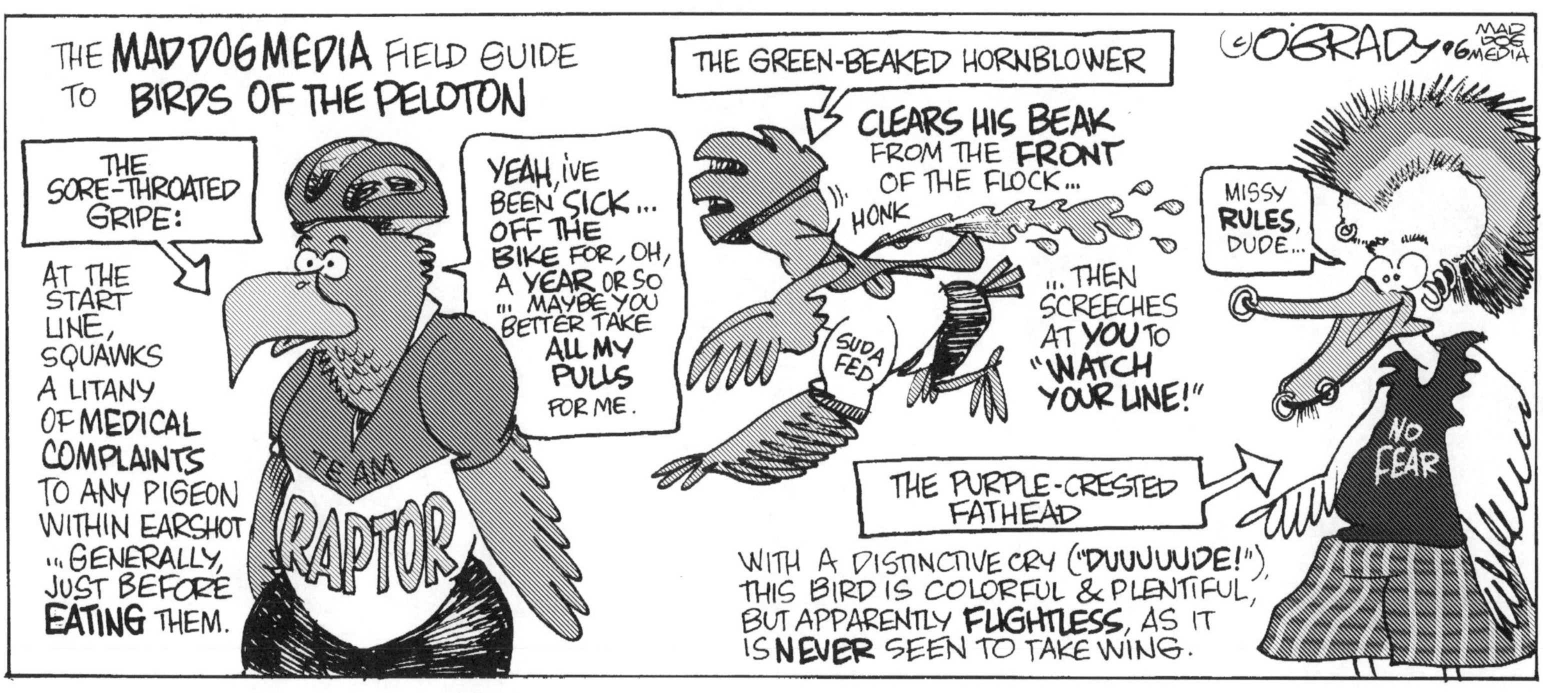
THE MAD DOG MEDIA FIELD GUIDE TO BIRDS OF THE PELOTON
©O'GRADY '96 MAD DOG MEDIA
THE SORE-THROATED GRIPE:
AT THE START LINE, SQUAWKS A LITANY OF MEDICAL COMPLAINTS TO ANY PIGEON WITHIN EARSHOT ... GENERALLY, JUST BEFORE EATING THEM.
YEAH, I'VE BEEN SICK ... OFF THE BIKE FOR, OH, A YEAR OR SO ... MAYBE YOU BETTER TAKE ALL MY PULLS FOR ME.
TEAM RAPTOR
THE GREEN-BEAKED HORNBLOWER
CLEARS HIS BEAK FROM THE FRONT OF THE FLOCK...
HONK
SUDA FED
... THEN SCREECHES AT YOU TO "WATCH YOUR LINE!"
MISSY RULES, DUDE...
NO FEAR
THE PURPLE-CRESTED FATHEAD
WITH A DISTINCTIVE CRY ("DUUUUUDE!"), THIS BIRD IS COLORFUL & PLENTIFUL, BUT APPARENTLY FLIGHTLESS, AS IT IS NEVER SEEN TO TAKE WING.

6-17-96 When all else fails, go for the funny animals.

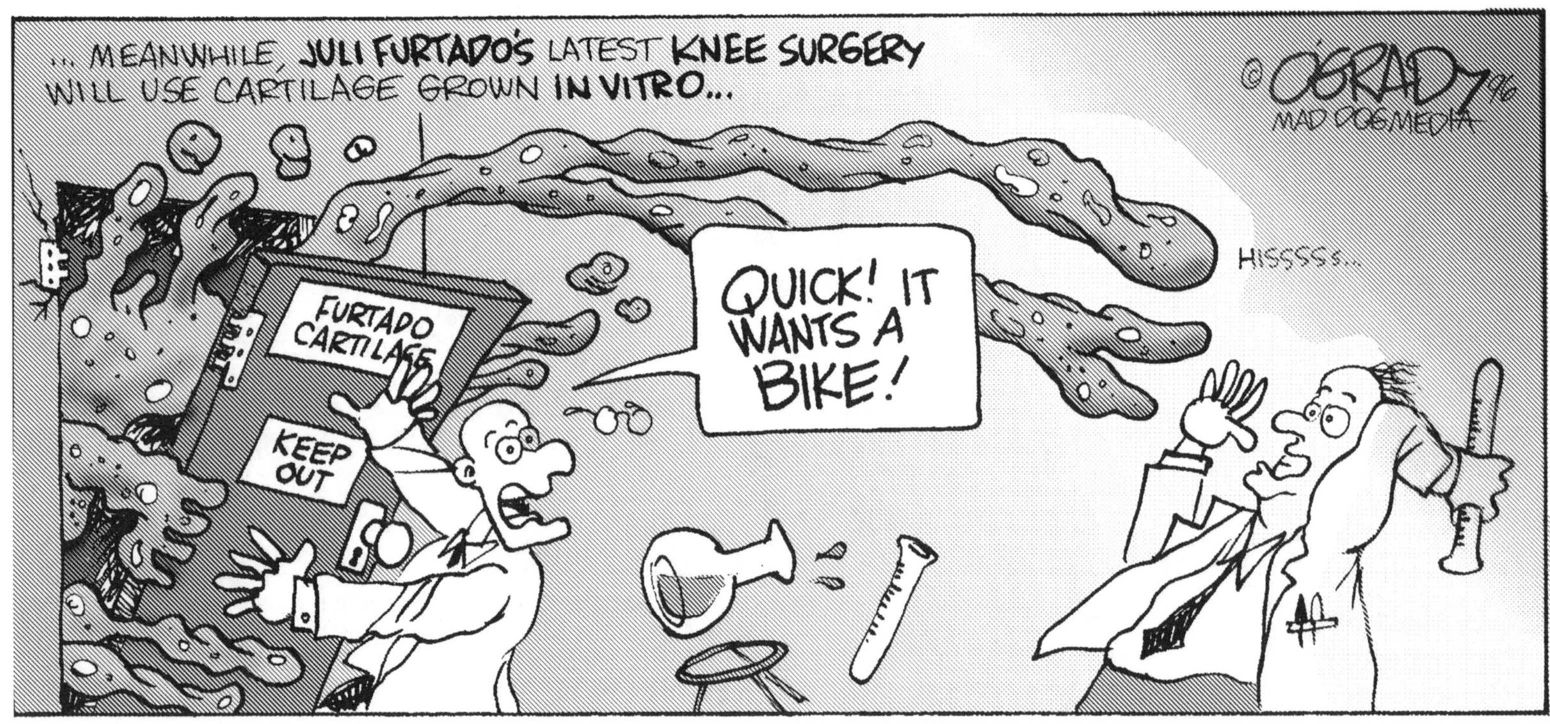
... MEANWHILE, JULI FURTADO'S LATEST KNEE SURGERY WILL USE CARTILAGE GROWN IN VITRO...
© O'GRADY '96 MAD DOG MEDIA
HISSSSS...
QUICK! IT WANTS A BIKE!
FURTADO CARTILAGE
KEEP OUT

10-28-96 Just think what you could get for that stuff on the black market.

©O'GRADY '97
MAD DOG MEDIA
... BUT THE REALLY SCARY THING WAS THAT HE WAS RIDING A MOUNTAIN BIKE!
... AND CARRYING A SACKFUL OF CASH...
ROAD TOADS
LEN PETTYJOHN
ANOTHER BIT OF ROAD KILL
R.I.P.
COORS CLASSIC
TOUR DUPONT

2-3-97 More science fiction: Len Pettyjohn is back, but this time with a mountain-bike race in Steamboat Springs, Colorado.

DUDE... THIS CACTUS CUP THING RULES! THERE'S LIKE BOOCOO SWAG, AND BABES, MAJORLY COOL STUFF AND LOTSA RAYS...
YEAH... AND I HEAR THERE'S EEVEN, LIKE, A RACE GOING ON AROUND HERE SOMEWHERES...
TOYZ
GASP
COUGH
HACK
WHEEZE

3-31-97 Sometimes the sideshow overshadows the main event. Cactus Cup-Westworld had all the appeal of a monster-truck rally.

THE POLO SPORT TEAM ENCOUNTERS SOME INITIAL RESISTANCE FROM MOUNTAIN BIKING'S TRADITIONALISTS...
YAAAHH! WEIRDO!
AINCHA GOT NO RESPECK F'TRADITION Y'BUM YEZ?
DON'T LOOK AT 'EM, ZAP...
AWW MOMMM...
POLO SPORT
SHAUN
THANKS TO CP
© O'GRADY MAD DOG MEDIA '97

4-14-97 Dese kids today. Look at 'im, will youse? Not a piercing or tat' on him anywheres. Jeez, what an oddball.

THE CURSE OF THE RAINBOW JERSEY...
HEY, HOW ABOUT GOING FOR A LITTLE RIDE?
... OF COURSE, YOU MIGHT CRASH...
THERE'S A RACE THIS WEEKEND, SO YOU'VE GOT TO TRAIN...
...BUT YOU'LL PROBABLY PUNCTURE...
WIN
WORLD CHAMPIONSHIP JERSEY & SHROUD
MAPEI GB
THAT'S IT... I'M GONNA SWITCH TO PRO GOLF...
DO YOU KNOW IF TIGER WOODS NEEDS A CADDY?
©O'GRADY '97 MAD DOG MEDIA

5-12-97 World champion Johan Museeuw was spending more time on the pavement than on the podium during the spring classics.

MEANWHILE, AT COLLEGIATE NATS...
I DON'T LIKE THE LOOK OF THESE CLOUDS...
USOL
UDNS
USOL
USOL
©O'GRADY '97
MAD DOG MEDIA

6-16-97 The Iron Hose strikes again: Snow pelted Durango's Iron Horse for the third year in a row, and this time the cops stopped the race, which this year was doing double duty as the collegiate national-championship road race.

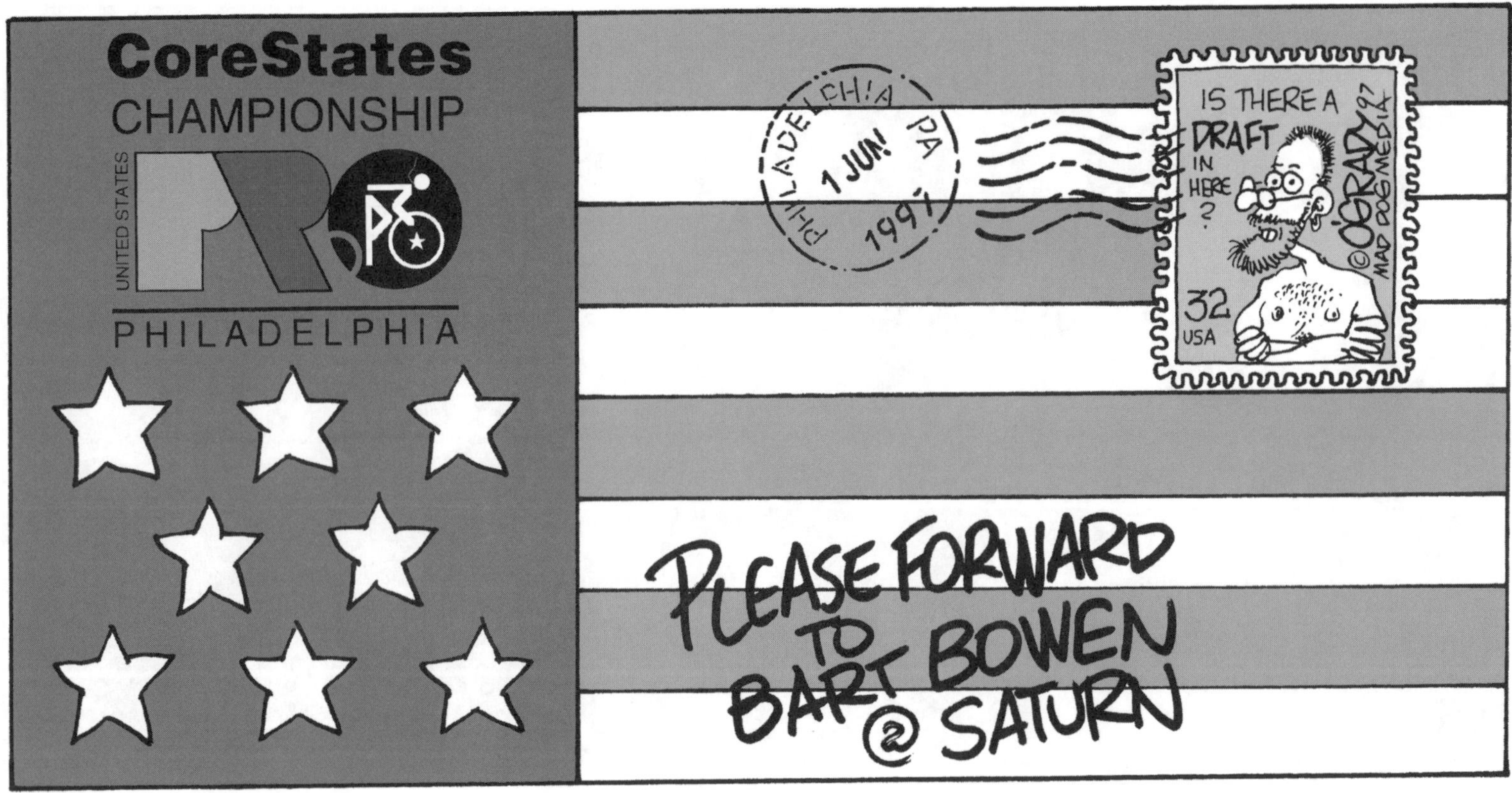

6-30-97 George Hincapie was stripped of his CoreStates win for allegedly motorpacing behind his team car after flatting nine miles from the finish. Bart Bowen wound up with the stars-and-stripes.

YEAH, IT'S BEEN GOING ON EVER SINCE THE TYSON-HOLYFIELD FIGHT...
... BETWEEN YOU AND ME, I'D JUST AS SOON THEY WENT BACK TO DOPE.
RRRR...
NNGHH
BUNS OF STEEL
BOB'S TOWING
ASS BANDITS
POLI GRIP
©O'GRADY 97
MAD DOG MEDIA

7-14-97 Hey, we'll hook you and bump you, even go on the juice…but we'll never bite one of your ears off. (The helmet gets in the way.)

BJARNE RIIS FACES THE PRESS AFTER THE DISNEYLAND TIME TRIAL...
BJARNE, WHAT HAPPENED OUT THERE TODAY? FALLING OVER AT SIGN-IN, MISSING YOUR START TIME, AND THAT INCIDENT INVOLVING THE BIKE CHANGE?
GAWRSH, I DUNNO ... I GUESS I JUST FELT A LITTLE GOOFY.
BUT I WON TH' BIKE TOSS...
HYUK
© O'GRADY '97 MAD DOG MEDIA
–APOLOGIES TO WALT D.

8-11-97 The 1997 Tour was hardly a trip to the Magic Kingdom for defending champ Bjarne Riis.

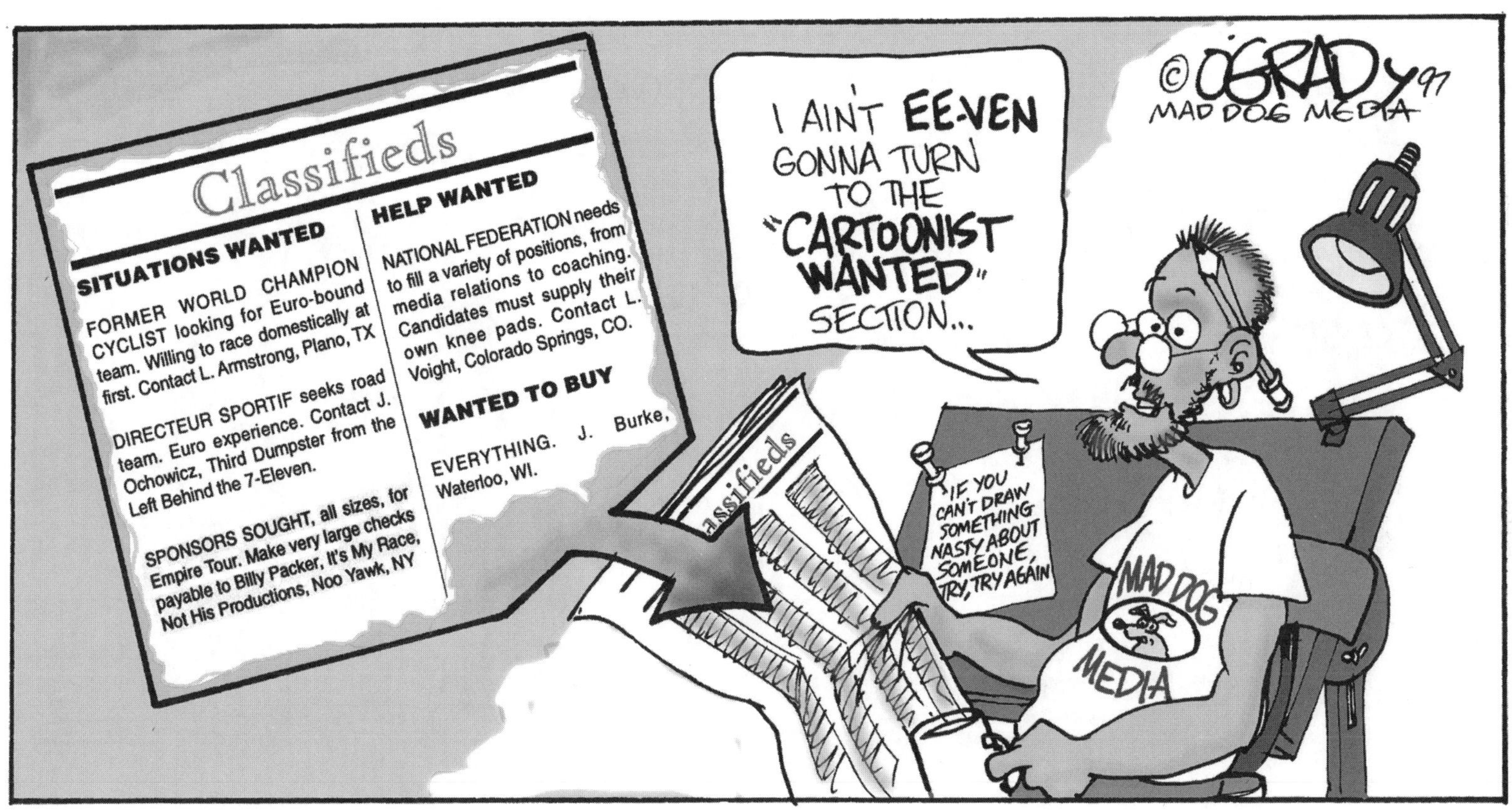
Classifieds
SITUATIONS WANTED
FORMER WORLD CHAMPION CYCLIST looking for Euro-bound team. Willing to race domestically at first. Contact L. Armstrong, Plano, TX
DIRECTEUR SPORTIF seeks road team. Euro experience. Contact J. Ochowicz, Third Dumpster from the Left Behind the 7-Eleven.
SPONSORS SOUGHT, all sizes, for Empire Tour. Make very large checks payable to Billy Packer, It's My Race, Not His Productions, Noo Yawk, NY
HELP WANTED
NATIONAL FEDERATION needs to fill a variety of positions, from media relations to coaching. Candidates must supply their own knee pads. Contact L. Voight, Colorado Springs, CO.
WANTED TO BUY
EVERYTHING. J. Burke, Waterloo, WI.
I AIN'T EE-VEN GONNA TURN TO THE "CARTOONIST WANTED" SECTION...
© O'GRADY 97 MAD DOG MEDIA
IF YOU CAN'T DRAW SOMETHING NASTY ABOUT SOMEONE, TRY, TRY AGAIN
MAD DOG MEDIA

10-6-97 If you thought the news was bad, wait 'til you see the classifieds.

CYCLO-CROSS SEASON AND WINTER HIT THE ROCKIES AT MORE OR LESS THE SAME TIME.
INTERESTING SNOWMAN, SON.
I DIDN'T BUILD HIM, DAD... HE'S BEEN HERE SINCE LAST SUNDAY.
IS IT L-L-LAST L-L-LAP YET?
©O'GRADY '97 MAD DOG MEDIA

11-17-97 At least the ice is soothing those nagging overuse injuries.

WHADDA I WANT FOR CHRISTMAS? HOW'BOUT MORE CLASS ACTS LIKE FURTADO AND ARMSTRONG AND FEWER FOOD-FIGHTING DOWNHILLERS?.. A REAL STAGE RACE TO REPLACE DU PONT? (WE'RE NOT TALKING "TOUR OF THE ROCKIES" HERE)... CARPAL TUNNEL FOR ALL TH' WANKERS ON @#!!*?!!! REC.BICYCLES.RACING... A LITTLE PRECISION EARTHQUAKE AT ONE OLYMPIC PLAZA IN COLORADO SPRINGS... A JALAPEÑO AND LSD ENEMA FOR EVERYONE AT THE UCI? AS MUCH TV TIME AS FIGURE SKATING... MORE JUNIORS AND FEWER MASTERS...
RANT RAVE ROAR
THIS IS WHY MRS. CLAUS AND I NEVER HAD KIDS.
MAD DOG MEDIA
VICIOUS LIL' 'TOONS
© O'GRADY 97
MAD DOG MEDIA

12-15-97 This is also why Shannon and I don't have any kids.

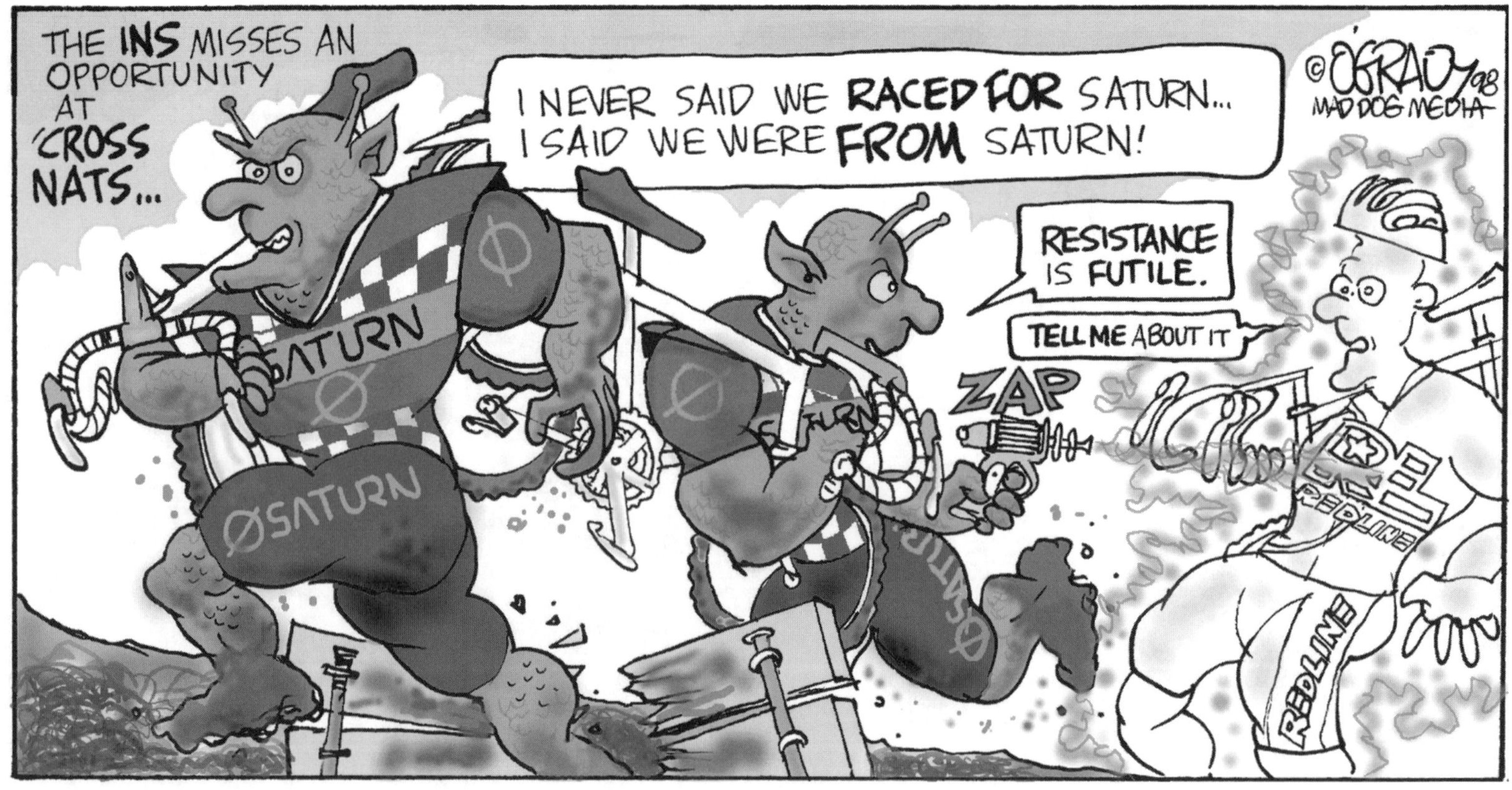
THE INS MISSES AN OPPORTUNITY AT 'CROSS NATS...
I NEVER SAID WE RACED FOR SATURN... I SAID WE WERE FROM SATURN!
RESISTANCE IS FUTILE.
TELL ME ABOUT IT
ZAP
©O'GRADY '98 MAD DOG MEDIA
SATURN
SATURN
REDLINE
REDLINE

1-12-98 The McCormack brothers seemed positively extraterrestrial, and the 'cross title stayed in the family for another year.

I'M TELLING YOU, IT'S THE BEEF!
OH, WE BELIEVE YOU, WE BELIEVE YOU...
... STILL, I'D START KEEPING THAT SKINSUIT ZIPPED ... OR BUY A CHEST RAZOR.
MAYBE I SHOULD LAY OFF THE PORK...
ITALIA
MUD STUD
OLD GUYS WHO GET FAT IN WINTER RACING TEAM
SPARE TIRE ALE
© GRADY '98 MAD COW MEDIA

22-98 Paola Pezzo was accused, then cleared, of doping with nandrolone. It was suggested that the positive tests could have been the result of consuming tainted beef.

YEEHAW!
TINKER'S SURE BEEN A LOT MORE COMPETITIVE SINCE CANNONDALE STARTED DOING MOTORCYCLES...
THANK GAWD HE AIN'T USIN' THE VOLVO...
BBBBBRRRRAPAPAPAPAP
©O'GRADY 98
MAD DOG MEDIA
THANKS TO HAL WALTER

3-30-98 Tinker's kicking butt; Cannondale's making motorcycles. Kinda makes you go, "Hmmm...."

CAN'T BEAR THE LAME COMMENTARY ON OUTDOOR LIFE'S RACE COVERAGE?
HERE ARE A FEW SOLUTIONS...
©O'GRADY 98 MAD DOG MEDIA

① ENJOY THE HIGH-QUALITY CYCLING COMMENTARY ON ABC, NBC, CBS AND FOX.
...TIGER WOODS...
CLICK
...MICHAEL JORDAN...
CLICK
...AL UNSER JR...
NOPE
NOPE
NOPE

② FILL THE VOID WITH YOUR OWN WELL-INFORMED INSIGHTS.
I WASN'T ACTUALLY AT THE RACE, BUT HERE'S WHAT I THINK HAPPENED BASED ON WHO I HEARD WAS GONNA BE THERE...
WELCOME TO WRECK. BICYCLES. RACING!
TAPPITY
TAPPITY
TAP

③ DRAG YOURSELF AWAY FROM THE TEEVEE AND GO FOR A NICE, LONG RIDE.
HE MAKES HIS MOVE ON THE STEEPEST HILL ON THE COURSE ... THE CROWD ROARS...

5-11-98 No good deed goes unpunished: The usual suspects were grumbling about the quality of Outdoor Life's cycling coverage.

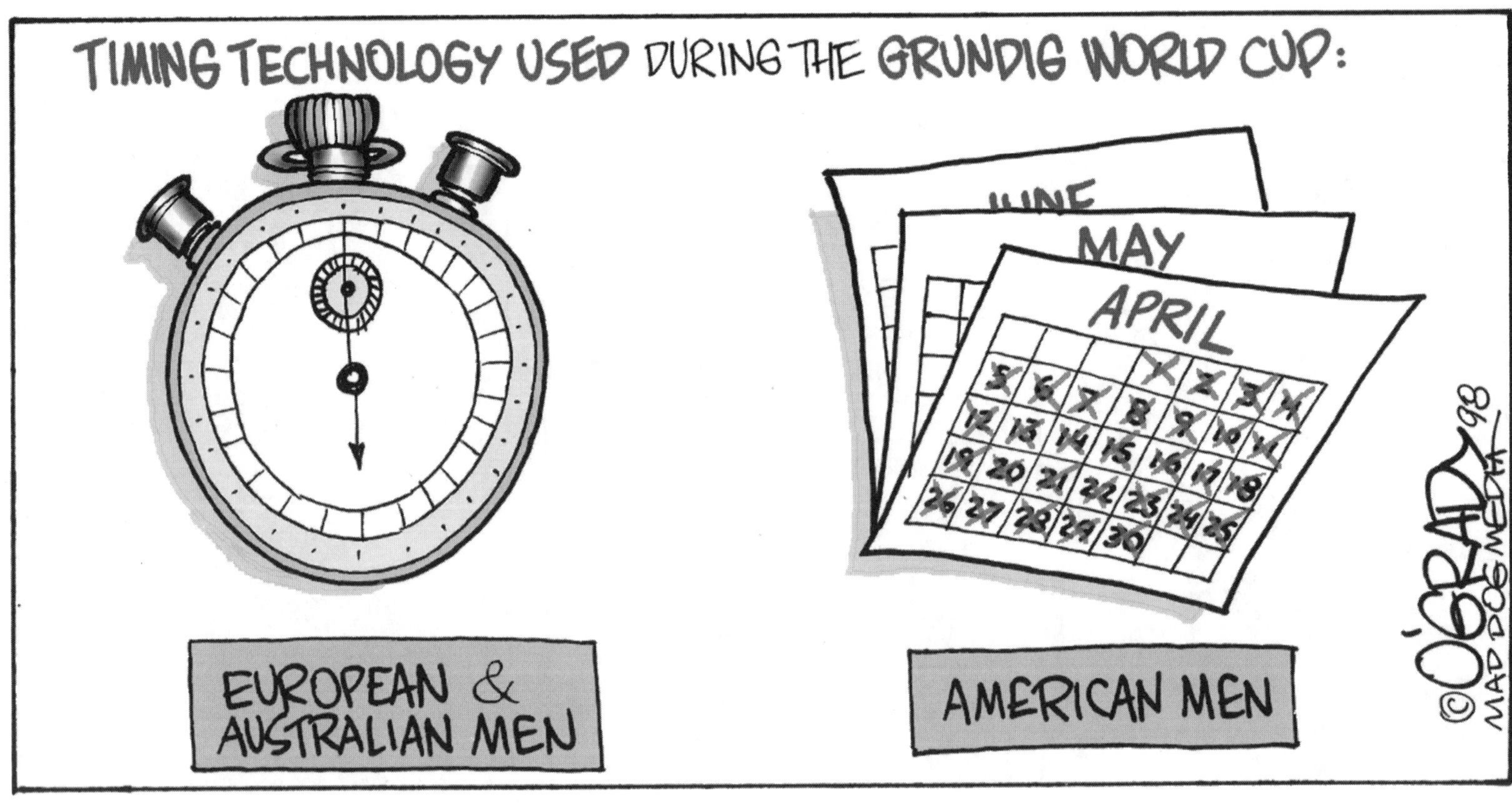

6-15-98 American men were finding the World Cup's upper echelons to be an exclusively Euro-Australian club.

ARCHAEOLOGISTS IN 2098 MAKE AN ASTOUNDING DISCOVERY...
WE THINK HE WAS SOME SORT OF TRIBAL CHIEFTAIN... THE "BIG BEAR."
NOTE THE VEHICLE... CLEARLY SUPERIOR TO THE FOUR-WHEELED BOXES USED BY THE MASSES...
2098? JEEZ... I GUESS A TOP-10 FINISH IS OUT OF THE QUESTION...
13 BIG BEAR
OTB SPORTS
©O'GRADY'98 MAD DOG MEDIA

6-29-98 This year, they should have changed the name to Polar Bear.

THE PAUSE THAT REFRESHES, TOUR STYLE...
THEY SAY THINGS GO BETTER WITH COKE... BUT THEY GO FASTER WITH EPO, 'ROIDS AND METH!
©O'GRADY '98
MAD DOG MEDIA
THANKS, CP
EPO
ROIDS
METH
NEEDLE EXCHANGE
FEED ZONE
MAIN LINE
HYPRO
MOTHER'S LITTLE HELPER
TRACKS

8-17-98 A doping scandal transformed the French Tour into The French Connection.

OBOY
OBOY
OBOY
Y'KNOW, I'D HEARD THAT CYCLING HAD A DRUG PROBLEM...
... BUT I HAD NO IDEA IT WAS THIS BAD...
BOG TROTTERS
BOING
©O'GRADY '98 MAD DOG MEDIA

9-21-98 Another kind of dope altogether enjoys running around in the mud, wearing a perfectly rideable bike.

ALLONS ENFANTS DE LA PATRIE, LE JOUR DE GLOIRE EST ARRIVÉ...
VIVE
LA
FRANCE
NOW I KNOW HOW THAT LIZARD FELT...
I WENT TO WORLD'S AND ALL I GOT WAS THIS STUPID T-SHIRT
USA
©O'GRADY '98 MAD DOG MEDIA

10-5-98 Take one French revolution at mountain-bike world's, blend with a popular beer and voila! Some bread and cheese with that whine, monsieur?

MEANWHILE, AT ROAD WORLDS...
YOU'RE A LITTLE EARLY FOR HALLOWEEN, KID... NO CANDY FOR YOU.
MUNCH MUNCH MUNCH
CUTE COSTUME, THOUGH... YOU LOOK JUST LIKE A BIKE RACER.
THANK THE NICE MAN AND LET'S GO, SON... DADDY HAS ANOTHER DULL COCKTAIL PARTY WITH HIS SPONSORS...
eüros
AMGEN
eüros
PFIZE
WORLD'S BEST #1 MEDALS
USA CYCLING
USA
2
3
©O'GRADY 98 MAD DOG MEDIA

10-26-98 You can't blame the spunky little guy on the trike. His home life's pretty tough, what with the evil stepdad and all.

©O'GRADY '99
MAD DOG MEDIA
HOLIDAY TURKEY...
I TELL YOU–I'M CLEAN! BUT EVERYONE IS AGAINST ME ... THEREFORE, I WILL QUIT CYCLING!
GOBBLE GOBBLE GOBBLE
GEE, DO YOU THINK WE'VE BEEN NEEDLING RICHARD TOO MUCH?
SOUNDS LIKE A HYPO-THETICAL QUESTION TO ME...
PRESS
PRESS
FESTINA
FESTINA

1-11-99 "Gobble gobble gobble," added Virenque, laying an egg that was immediately impounded by police.

THEY SAY IT WAS COLD IN POPRAD, BUT IT'S FROZEN OVER IN HELL.
©O'GRADY '99
MAD DOG MEDIA
CONGRATULATIONS, GUYS!
WILL RACE FOR FOOD MEDALS!
IOU USA CYCLIN
USA
1
3

3-1-99 Finally, some good news for a change: Matt Kelly and Tim Johnson take the junior gold and under-23 bronze at cyclo-cross world's, America's first-ever 'cross medals.

I HEAR THE TEAM DIRECTOR BROUGHT BILL WOODUL UP...
YEAH... WHAT WITH OLD EARTHQUAKE JAKE UP HERE NOW, WE NEED THE BEST TECH SUPPORT WE CAN GET...
O'GRADY '99
© MAD DOG MEDIA
PEARLY GATES VELO
ZOOM
WHOOPS
BOING
BASH
CLATTER
BILL!
COMING, JAKE... YOU STAY AWAY FROM LUCIFER'S DOWNHILL COURSE, NOW...

4-19-99 Heaven must have some great riding; all our best people seem to end up there. This time, it was Bill Woodul and "Earthquake" Jake Watson.

Back to the Old Drawing Board

Night of the Living 'Toon

There's a reason cartoonists sketch their ideas in pencil first. It's called Darwinism: Some 'toons must die so that others may live. Starting off in easily erased No. 2H Kimberly lets you thin the herd without remorse.

THE OTHER OLYMPIC BOMB...
WHEW... MY EARS'RE RINGING...
...WHY, I CAN'T EVEN HEAR THE APPLAUSE!
PROJECT 96
USA CYCLING
©O'GRADY 96
MADDOGMEDIA
This cartoon about the "success" of USA Cycling's Project 96 never made it into print. I still think it's funny. Mean and insensitive, but funny.

After inking with a series of technical pens, a 'toon is harder to abort. And once it's scanned and colored via a senile MacClone, a digital D&C is out of the question; the 'toon is a member of the family.

Before you know it, you've got some serious time and effort invested in the little guy, from conception through birth, to nurturing and correction. Once it's finally ready to leave home for a job at one magazine or another, you've come to like it more than somewhat, maybe even love it.

And no matter how acute you believe your perception to be in other matters, a cartoonist will never admit that his baby is ugly.

That's what editors are for.

An editor will not only tell you your baby is ugly, he will suggest that it may be mentally defective, humor-impaired or criminally insane. Maybe all three. Set this two-dimensional Quasimodo to scampering around the battlements of the editorial page and we'll shed readers and advertisers like a dead dog sheds fleas, he'll say.

So you plead your case, arguing and objecting like a public defender battling a sharp DA. If you're lucky, you get a continuance, and your boy gets another chance down the road. Maybe you win on appeal. But nine times out of 10, it's Life in the Filing Cabinet Without Possibility of Parole.

Still, society being what it is, there are more seriously twisted cartoons than there are filing cabinets to hold them. We need the space for the truly vicious libels. So the filing cabinet's drawers are flung open and the misdemeanor gags shamble forth, free at last, blinking at the light, toward a chance at honest work for the first time anywhere, this time in the pages of a book.

Hey, see that ugly little bastard over there, the one about the '96 Olympics? That's my boy.

Q. WHAT DO YOU GET WHEN YOU CROSS A CYCLING TEAM WITH THE U.S. POSTAL SERVICE?

A. A BIKE RACER WHO TAKES FOREVER TO GET WHERE HE'S GOING, IS ALL MESSED UP WHEN HE ARRIVES, AND WANTS MORE MONEY.

TH' RACE'S OVER? YEST'RDAY? HEY, DUDE, THAT WAS A FED'RAL HOLIDAY NO RACIN' ON FED'RAL HOL'DAYS...
NOW GIMME SOME @#!!!☆?! PRIZE MONEY OR I'LL SHOOT YA.
US
POSTAL CYCLING TEAM
MAD DOG MEDIA

1995 Our mail carrier had been shredding my copies of *VeloNews*, and this may have been my way of getting even. It didn't work: The 'toon was never printed, she's still shredding my mags, and two years later she upped the ante by running over my dog.

THE U.S. POSTAL SERVICE BRINGS ITS PARTICULAR STRENGTHS TO CYCLING...
WELL I AIN'T RACING ON NO @#!!! FEDERAL HOLIDAYS!
YEAH, AND I WANT MORE MONEY!
IF YOU GUYS DON'T SHUT UP I'M GONNA... NNGH... RRR...
©BRAY '95 MAD DOG MEDIA
US
USPS

1995 Another shot at the same target. "Going postal" had become part of the language, so I thought it might fly. VN thought otherwise.

THANK YOU, MA'AM ... MAY I HAVE ANOTHER?
ONLY IF YOU PROMISE NOT TO TELL, YOU NAUGHTY GIRL, YOU...
DISCIPLINARY BOARD
TWIGG
USA CYCLING
© O'GRADY '96 MAD DOG MEDIA

1996 Another take on the Rebecca Twigg-USA Cycling plea bargain and gag order following the Atlanta Games.

1996 Chris Horner would not make the Olympic team, and this cartoon would not make Page 7.

WELL ... WHADDAYA THINK?
I THINK YOU OUGHT TO FLUSH IT.
© O'GRADY 96 MAD DOG MEDIA
USA CYCLING
PROJECT 96
GO USA WIN GOLD

1996 A meaner comment on the '96 Olympics.

OUCH!
OUCH!
OUCH!
OUCH!
OUCH!
OUCH!
LE TOUR '96
©O'GRADY '96
MAD DOG MEDIA

1996 I thought the 1996 Tour was a meat grinder, and I still like this 'toon.

OK, THERE'S THIS GUY ON THE UCI MANAGEMENT COMMITTEE, AND WHEN HE DIES, HE GOES UP TO ST. PETER, AND THEN...
SORRY, BUDDY, BUT NOBODY GETS IN WIDDOUT A TOP TUBE... THEM'S TH' RULES.
SHRIEK!
HI THERRE...sss WE'VE BEEN EXPECTING YOU HISSSS
PUNT
SECURITY
PEARLY GATES INC. A DIVISION OF TREK BICYCLES
© O'GRADY 97 MAD DOG MEDIA

1997 The UCI kept handing down commandments, making life hell for bike designers. I thought they should reap as they sowed.

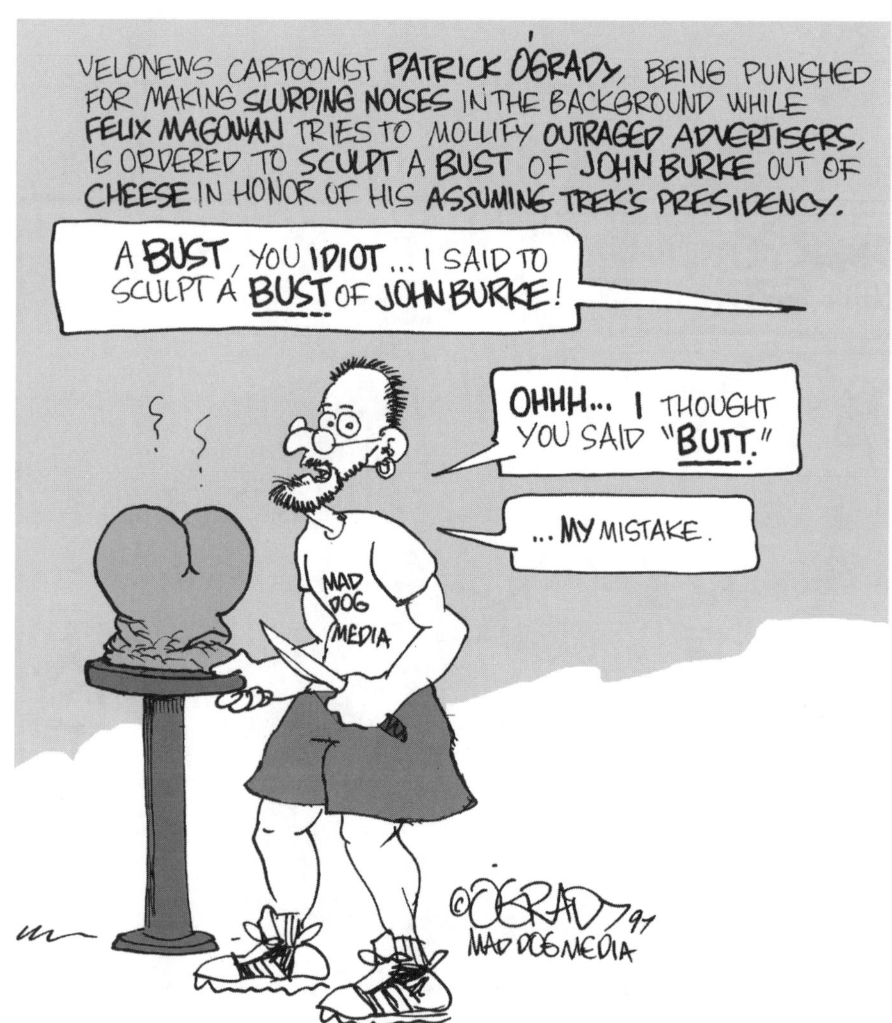
VELONEWS CARTOONIST PATRICK O'GRADY, BEING PUNISHED FOR MAKING SLURPING NOISES IN THE BACKGROUND WHILE FELIX MAGOWAN TRIES TO MOLLIFY OUTRAGED ADVERTISERS, IS ORDERED TO SCULPT A BUST OF JOHN BURKE OUT OF CHEESE IN HONOR OF HIS ASSUMING TREK'S PRESIDENCY.
A BUST, YOU IDIOT... I SAID TO SCULPT A BUST OF JOHN BURKE!
OHHH... I THOUGHT YOU SAID "BUTT."
...MY MISTAKE.
MAD DOG MEDIA
©O'GRADY 97 MAD DOG MEDIA

1997 VN's advertising director asked if I would do a humorous card for John Burke to commemorate his ascendancy at Trek. And if someone gives him a copy of this book, he'll finally get a look at it.

THEY SAY IT'S A FLOWER POT, AND BEAUTIFUL THINGS WILL GROW IN IT...
WELL, IT SURE SMELLS LIKE FERTILIZER TO ME...
BRAC
REGIONAL REP PROGRAM
MAD DOG MEDIA
©O'GRADY '98 MAD DOG MEDIA

1998 The Bicycle Racing Association of Colorado thought USA Cycling's regional-rep program stunk.

I TELL YIS, IT'S A DELICIOUS STEW...
... AND YIS CAN EAT IT OR BEAT IT!
DON'T WAIT UP...
USA CYCLING
REGIONAL REP PROGRAM
RACERS & RACES
© CARTER '98 MAD DOG MEDIA

1998 An even less appetizing approach to the same topic.

BOOOO
HISSS
HISS
AND THE WINNER OF THE MISS USAC PAGEANT IS... MISS REGIONAL REP!
MISS REGIONAL REP
BOOO
PFFBBLLL
GWAAAN
GEDOUTA
HEEYAH
BBBRAZZZ
THERRRE SHE ISSSS... MISS YOOOOESSSAAASEE...
DUDE... SOMEBODY NEEDS GLASSES.
FILL MINE WITH WHISKEY.
phat hedz
ROAD
TOADS
©98 O'GRADY MAD DOG MEDIA

1998 The USAC staffer charged with pushing the regional-rep program was a pageant competitor. She wasn't exactly Miss Congeniality at a BRAC-USAC meeting to discuss the program, I had a deadline, and shazam! Another one bites the dust.

BE WITH YA INNA MINUTE, HON...
GWAN, GO RIDE YA BIKE OR SOMPIN... CANTCHA SEE MOMMY HAS A SPONSOR?
AND TAKE THAT MUTT TO TH' POUND!
ARF?
US AC
GRASS ROOTS CYCLING
DIST REPS
©GRADY '98 MAD DOG MEDIA

1998 I felt USA Cycling was being short-sighted in concentrating on elite programs and sponsorship to the detriment of long-term goals like grass-roots athlete development. I still do.

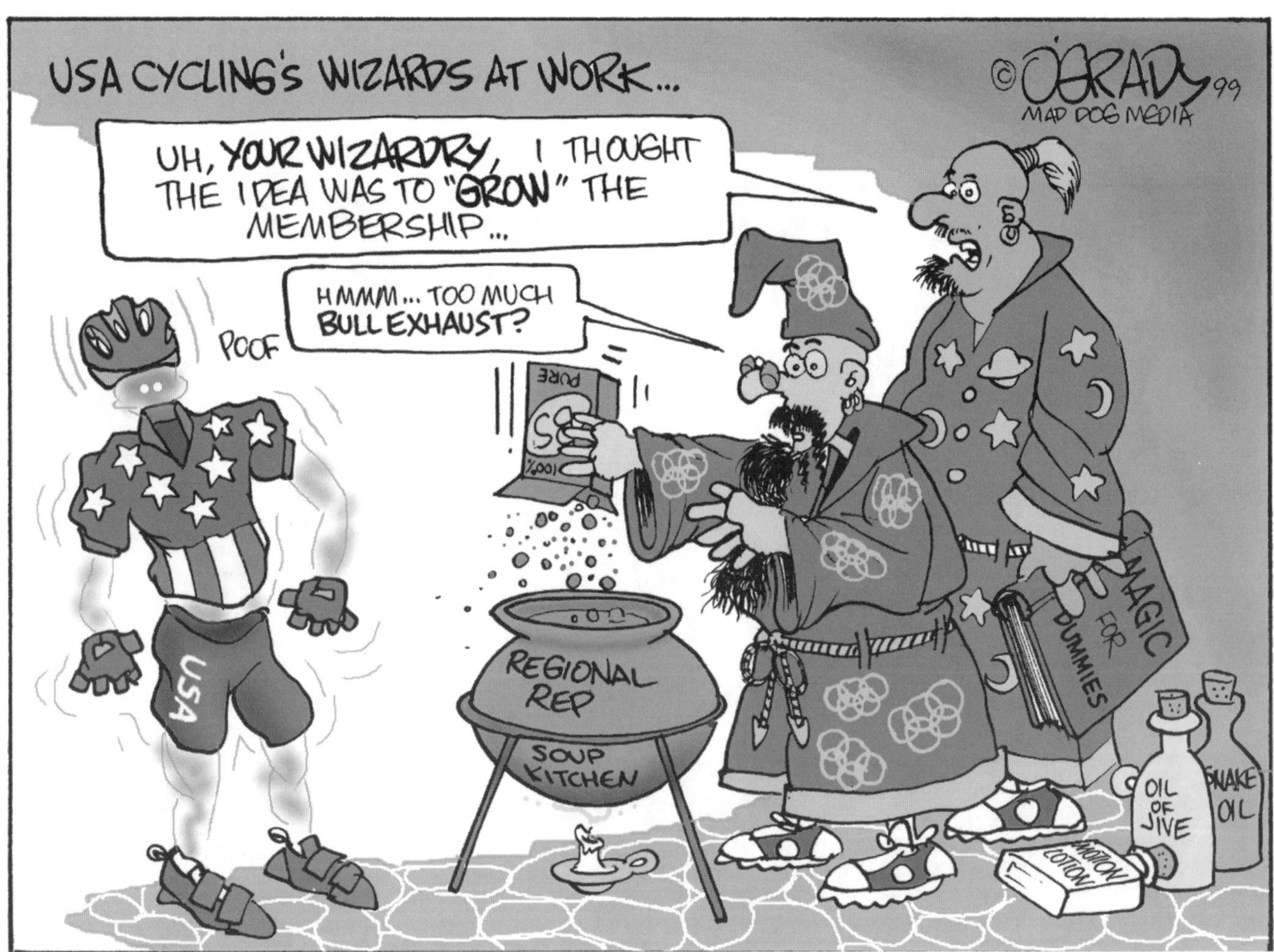
USA CYCLING'S WIZARDS AT WORK...
© O'GRADY 99
MAD DOG MEDIA
UH, YOUR WIZARDRY, I THOUGHT THE IDEA WAS TO "GROW" THE MEMBERSHIP...
HMMM... TOO MUCH BULL EXHAUST?
POOF
PURE
100%
USA
REGIONAL REP
SOUP KITCHEN
MAGIC FOR DUMMIES
OIL OF JIVE
SNAKE OIL
MOTION LOTION

1999 The editors wanted more serious journalism on USA Cycling, but fewer vicious cartoons. It was kind of like shooting puppies at the pound—in short, hardly sporting—but I kept doing it anyway.

USA
CYCLING
NO ADMITTANCE
DON'T SAY WE NEVER FERTILIZE THEM GRASS ROOTS!
HAHAHAHAHAH HAHAHAHAHAH
MORE CHAMPAGNE
SO THAT'S HOW THEY KEEP THE MOAT FULL...
USA
©O'GRADY '99
MAD DOG MEDIA

1999 An awfully elaborate, Monty Pythonesque toilet joke about Fortress USAC, which had refused to grant *VeloNews* an interview with CEO Lisa Voight to discuss the association's direction and goals.

WHAT THE ME ARE YOU, SOME KIND OF A WISEGUY?
SORRY ABOUT THAT, DUDE
© O'GRADY '99 MAD DOG MEDIA CONGRATULATIONS, GUYS!
USA

1999 One of the editors didn't get this "hell freezes over" limper about the U.S. success at 'cross worlds. Just as well; the one that ran was a better cartoon.

MEANWHILE, IN ARIZONA...
I'M NOT DEAD YET...
UH HUH, YEAH, OK, WHATEVER ... BY ANY CHANCE, DO YOU KNOW WHEN THE NEXT BUS TO MONTEREY LEAVES?
WELCOME TO CACTUS CUP
THE INDUSTRY
©O'GRADY 99
MAD DOG MEDIA

1999 Another editor argued that this was unfair because the first Specialized-free Cactus Cup wasn't intended to be a marquee event like Sea Otter. My intent was to note the industry's apparent lack of interest in a once-great race.

Pedigree

Patrick O'Grady is, in a word, unemployable.

Before suffering a brief attack of clarity in 1991, during which he finally deciphered the career-track graffiti sprayed on the brick wall of daily journalism, the peripatetic writer, editor and cartoonist had spent some 15 years staggering throughout the American West in search of the perfect newspaper job—high pay, low work load and a boss who was both out of sight and out of his (or her) mind.

Gigs like that were not to be found at fish-wrappers like the *Colorado Springs Sun*, the Colorado Springs *Gazette Telegraph*, *The Arizona Daily Star* in Tucson, the *Corvallis* (Oregon) *Gazette-Times*, the *Pueblo* (Colorado) *Chieftain* and *The New Mexican* in Santa Fe—unless you were a publisher, a managing editor or the owner.

But O'Grady finally found two of his three requirements (guess which) in the shadowy world of free-lancing. And despite the Supreme Court's many rulings regarding community standards and pornography, his articles, columns and cartoons about cycling have desecrated the pages of a number of publications, many of which, surprisingly, remain in business today: *VeloNews*, *Inside Triathlon*, *Bicycle Retailer & Industry News*, *Wintersport Business*, *Dirt Rag*, *Outdoor Retailer*, *Mountain Biker*, *Bike*, the *Gazette Telegraph*, the *Seattle Post-Intelligencer*, *USA Today Online*, *Rocky Mountain Sports*, *InLine* and *Yahoo! Internet Life*, to name a few.

A rabid cyclo-crosser who often can be seen lumbering past disbelieving deer near his home in the Wet Mountains of south-central Colorado, the balding, bespectacled 45-year-old ne'er-do-well helps promote a 'cross or two from time to time. In 1996, he helped edit the second edition of Simon Burney's classic work on the sport, *Cyclo-cross*. And in 1997, he lent a hand to the U.S. Cyclo-cross National Championships near Golden, Colorado, a labor of lunacy that, despite his best efforts, resulted in neither deaths nor dismemberments.

Between obscene phone calls to libel lawyers, trips to the liquor store and futile attempts to hide checks from his long-suffering wife, Shannon, O'Grady uploads surplus vitriol to the Mad Dog Media ArfNet, a Web site unsullied by any notions of editorial control or fair play (www.ris.net/~velodog). *The Season Starts When?* is his first book.